Rejoice, O young man, in your youth; an
the days of your youth, and walk in the w
   sight of your eyes: but know you, that for all these things God will
bring you into judgment. So, banish sorrow from your heart, and cast-
   off pain from your body, for youth and vigour are fleeting.

Ecclesiastes 11:9

Simon,

A valued & trusted colleague

enjoy the morning read

Introduction

I have written this before my memory fades or my brief time on this earth runs its course, also for the many ex-soldiers who I hope can relate to this simple re telling of perhaps in some way, their own initial military experiences.

I have also written it for those who have never served within the Armed forces in any branch but think the Armed forces was an easy option to the high unemployment rates in the late 1970s, early 80s.

This memoir is in no way a hundred percent accurate in its timeline of events. It can seem tedious at times, but I am trying to show the diligence that shaped us. However, being written 45 years later I claim a small allowance must be made for my fading memory.

However, the fact remains that the events here unfolded for you left such an impression on upon my life that I feel an overwhelming compulsion to re tell them these 45 years later, this is my first-year training in the Coldstream Guards.

I want to acknowledge my thanks to; Major (Retired) Steve Cook. RM. SBS for writing the foreword.

Gary Fish

Forword by

Major (Retired) Steve Cook.

Royal Marines, Special Boat Squadron.

I have known the Author for several years, I have not served with him, as I am a Royal Marine, not a Guardsman. However, both professional Soldiers. This is not a dry and yawning history of the Coldstream Guards, of which there are many, and probably many to follow. Neither a Special Forces blockbuster.

It will remind Enlisted men and Officers of the hard graft of initial training, and the further training utilised in later deployments. The ridiculous and those things which seemed perverse but became practical when "things kicked off". Some of them remaining ridiculous.

This book is a narrative, written without humour, but the most humorous piece many of us will pull from a shelf. What Gary describes, is an environment that a lot of us faced daily. It explains and makes plain what we were dealing with, Sore feet and decent breakfast being the highlight, with a linear depreciation as the days progressed.

The days turning into weeks, weeks turning into months. It might also explain to Partners, Sons and Daughters, or interlopers, why we did it.

Dedicated to the officers, other ranks of the Household Division who burned leather, with a spoon, candle and Kiwi polish in the Brigade Squad, Caterham company, Junior Guardsman company, Junior leaders, in both Caterham & Pirbright Guards Depot.

CONTENTS

Chapter

Chapter I

Norfolk

I have always had an affinity for the sea and the coast; it is not from any long-drawn-out family tradition of fishermen or naval servitude; in fact, my known lineage is centred on the Derbyshire dales. It is simply that I grew up with the smell of the sea in my nose all my adolescent life.

I have lived sporadically in various places all over the world, but I am always drawn back to Norfolk because of my family. It is though more than that, it is the lure of the sea. I can remember the summer months in the village of Hemsby, just north of Great Yarmouth; I shared a room with my two younger brothers even though we had seven bedrooms in the former Victorian village blacksmiths in which we used to live.

The windows were always left wide open by my mum during the summer, the sun would appear to shine forever in those seemingly endless days of the latter 1970`s. A few hundred meters away from our house was Hemsby Village church. It was typical of the style of medieval church you find in Norfolk in that it was covered in large pieces of flint mixed in with the stone.

I could always see a glimpse of the church's clock face from my bedroom window as my bed was placed in such a way that the high and central church spire which displayed the clock was facing our house and was perfectly in line with my window. It was a great feeling, in the cloudless days during the summer, to watch the time go by whilst daydreaming on my bed.

It was mesmerising at times to watch the hands of that clock, as if they were being tentatively pushed by an invisible hand that moved them from one-minute marker to the next. I would wait at times, as it hovered between the minutes, staring intently, and wondering if it would move; of course, it always did. Even though the beach and sea were a good two miles away, the salty sea air would meander into our bedroom on the occasional breeze. The overall combination of the clock and the warm sea air would leave me with a sense of wellbeing and security. I knew then, even at my young age, that it was a timeless feeling, and I still reflect on that as I write here today.

It was on a chilly September morning that I woke up to the smell of that sea air making its way through the gaps in the frame of the old-fashioned sash windows of my room, the chill and the sea smell interrupted occasionally by the smell of freshly cut bacon from the village Butchers that was being cooked by my Old Man. It was five O'clock in the morning, September the 11th 1979. I was just sixteen years and 4 months old; I was filled with an emotional mixture of excitement, anticipation, and dread at what this day meant, now that it had finally arrived. Today was the day I joined the army.

The suitcase was thrown into the back of the van my old man used to sell potatoes door to door. I sat on a 55lb bag of King Edwards in my best and only suit, which had been newly bought from the sale at Burton's in Great Yarmouth market place the day before.

I had never worn a suit until that morning. I had never worn any of the new underpants my mum had bought for me from the marketplace either, a purchase unbeknown to me until I opened the pack at five in the morning and saw that they were very badly made seconds! All my old underpants had been thrown away by my mother who wanted me to have new and top quality, which is why she had borrowed money from my grandparents to buy the suit, socks, underpants, wash bag, sewing kit and suitcase. She had arranged the small buffet meal for my family

8

to bid me farewell in the first and last pub in Caister-On-Sea the night before.

My mother had faithfully bought all the items listed in the letter that the Army careers office had sent. The underpants were at least size 60 waists. I cursed as I tried them on as best I could; even though I was a bit chubby I was only a size 36. The solution I came up with was to tie a knot either side at the waist and another at the crotch to make them tighter and fit without falling, it did not matter how silly they looked after all, whoever sees you in your underpants.

The knot I had tied to the crotch of my new super king-size underpants was very irritating as I bumped up and down on my sack of 'spuds' in the back of the van during the short journey to Great Yarmouth station. The knot was a decision I was now beginning to regret; also, irritating me further, was the two ten-pound notes each of which was folded and securely cello-taped to the inside bridge of both my feet. This oddity was done on the advice of the village Vicar who had travelled outside Norfolk extensively, including years of living in London.

The vicar was a regular visitor to our house in the weeks prior to my leaving for the Army. I remember, with affection, how enthusiastic he was about my trip and future. The directions he gave were so precise the whole family knew the route from Liverpool Street station to Waterloo via the underground and ultimately to the Guards depot Pirbright Surrey.

I always find The Dirty Dozen, in the film of the same name, amusing when I watch the scenes of them reciting in unison the various tasks, and places for the intended attack on the Chateau. The difference being that in our house, instead of Lee Marvin overseeing the briefings, the vicar would stand with eyes slightly closed, as though he had just arrived in Liverpool Street station himself and describe the route. After each description, my family and I would all recite the same words back to him. However, instead of a collection of differing regional American accents, the front room resounded with the sound of six broad Norfolk burrs.

The journey began only after an embarrassing and lengthy emotional farewell from my mother who constantly repeated that I should bury my pride if I did not like the Army and come home, little did she know that in my mind it did not matter what they would do to me I was never coming back to Norfolk. I knew full well how that would end up with me working in a garden centre or an amusement arcade in the summer, or worse still unemployed. Norfolk then, as today, is a high unemployment area.

I had already worked in an amusement arcade from the age of 14 every summer during the school holidays to get money for my mum to buy my school uniform each term and to put away some money for me to use in the winter for the youth club etc. Working in an amusement arcade as a teenager was one thing but to think of it as a full-time job was another. In any case, my mother should have known in her heart I would not quit. She knew from my earliest years as far back as I could remember that I had always said I wanted to be in the Army.

This really, upon reflection, was not that strange as my father, uncles, great uncles, grandfather, great grandfathers on both sides of my family had all been in the military, mostly in the Army. It is fair to say that the Army was, to coin the phrase, in my blood.

When I was five, I went missing from my mother's guest house in Rodney Rd Great Yarmouth. It was only after a failed frantic search by all the guests and neighbours of the nearby surrounding areas that I was eventually found and returned home by the police. The police officers told my mother that they had found me on the seafront. I was, according to family accounts, annoyed at the police apparently claiming that I was off to join the Army as the Japanese were going to kill us all.

This fear of the Japanese, I now understand, was a follow up reaction to an event which occurred at my first Chinese meal, in the first Chinese restaurant, moreover, the first foreign food outlet other than fish and chips in Great Yarmouth. The family story is that I was constantly knocking the food out my brother's mouth and exclaiming to all the diners in the restaurant that the food was poisoned. Did nobody but me realise the Japanese were the enemy? I would scream and beg everyone entering the restaurant to run back out and call the Marines to rescue us, I think I watched to many John Wayne war films as a child.

It was after a very emotional farewell that the train made its way across the reclaimed piece of marshland used for the track towards Norwich. I distinctly remember, as is often the case in these instances that become burned into all our memories that a moment of clarity came over me.

My senses were as sharp as the bitter breeze coming through the small half open carriage window. I had an overwhelming feeling of Loss as familiar places passed me by through the window in which I could see my own reflection in the fading moonlight. The glow of the streetlights in the holiday park opposite which seemed to dance across the rain covered brilliant white caravan rooftops of the familiar but now departing out of view Vauxhall Caravan Park.

The reassuring and steadfast water tower in Caister also came into view, reassuring to me because my granddad had told me it had been a marker or reference point for returning American aviators during WWII. The poignancy of that was not lost upon me then thinking of exactly what that tower must have meant to those men, not just a reference point but also a symbol of safety and familiarity in an uncertain unfamiliar world. It too soon faded into the distance.

In Norwich I changed trains, the comparison of the smart London bound train against the bumpy, bouncy, aging carriages of the Great Yarmouth to Norwich one made the latter look extremely decrepit. I remember looking on this as a positive; old was behind me, new was ahead, and the feeling of anxiety I had been keeping under control seemed to suddenly drift away.

I was able, for the first time in quite a while, to smile to myself as I boarded and I recalled the occasions and words of Jack London, the Headmaster at my school Martham secondary modern. He had, on more than one occasion, delighted at seeing me outside his Headmasters' door as I pretended not to care about the inevitable and searing stinging pain, he would soon be metering out to me with, what was termed then "six of the best" which was to be inflicted upon my poor backside, or my upturned hand the choosing of which was dependent, I suppose, on his mood. In any case, on entering his office you would see him smile and grin in the anticipation of doling out justice.

I specifically remembered one of these Victorian styled disciplinary sessions in his office where Jack had decided that "six of the best" on my backside was the suitable punishment for my bunking off school and not returning after the mid-morning break. I had fancied a wander around Martham village instead, but a Villager had spotted me, and frog marched me back to school. In those good old days, you did what adults told you to, especially when held by the scruff of the neck. These days, any member of the public would likely be assaulted or reported by a pupil for doing the same.

In any instance, the severity of carrying out the caning left Jack with the saliva dribbling from the corner of his mouth, his three or four strands of combe over Brylcream-encrusted hair stood up straight from his now semi exposed bald head, it was in between deep pants of breath, which he took to recover his lost composure, that he then asked me the question I supposed all teachers or parents eventually ask.

"What are you going to do with your life Fish, as you're a no good, come on tell me what a day dreamer like you think you can achieve in your life ...?"

To which I replied, trying to conceal tears and the quiver in my voice,

"Join thaaaar...mey loik moi oile maaan sir",

(For those not from Norfolk! "Join the army like my father.")

I could remember him then, just like that as I stood in Norwich station, as I waited for the train to leave, also saying to me with creamy white spittle congealing at the corners of his mouth,

"You won't last five minutes Fish... you're no good, you have no self-discipline, you're lazy, and worst of all you're as thick as two short planks now get out of my office!

I had a large smile on my face, which was brought about by my newfound optimism for the future, coupled with successfully breaching the boundaries of Great Yarmouth as far as Norwich! Moreover, making the distance of the forty or so meters from one platform to the other in the big city station without being mugged, stripped of my nice new suit, or left for dead by the side of the track gave me the confidence to swear to myself that I would prove that sadistic old pervert wrong.

I eventually arrived in London Liverpool Street station. My first thoughts were "what a dirty old dump", as I set off dragging the weight of my suitcase towards the exit manned ticket barrier. I was suddenly and unwittingly un-prepared to see what I now could see ahead, the first Black person in the flesh. I had seen Black people of course in films and books but here this was a real live Black man.

I write this not wishing to come across as a racist, but because I want to show how insular we, my family, and friends in Hemsby, Great Yarmouth, and I believe Norfolk in general were. As I write this, I feel a flush of embarrassment at how ignorant I must have looked staring at that poor man for what seemed like ages.

It was time to get my instructions out and the vicar was spot on, apart from letting the first tube that arrived depart without me as I was to slow and apprehensive of the closing doors, I eventually arrived at Waterloo station bewildered as to why there had been no underground Bank at, Bank Station?

Waterloo station was gigantic compared to Great Yarmouth and Norwich and it was also bustling with people who were all rushing back and forth in every direction. I had never seen so many people in one place, not even in Great Yarmouth on Market Day.

I went to the middle of the station where hundreds of people were all stood looking up towards the train information boards. I was in awe at the flapping noise from the information boards that were changing so fast as the details changed and updated in what seemed like an instant. As soon as a platform number came up for a given destination, a throng of people that had been stood still around me one minute quickly headed as one in the direction of that platform. It seemed to me so

14

technical that the destinations were listed all over southeast & the southwest of England.

My train was ultimately going to Southampton via Brookwood where I had to get off for the oddly named Guards Depot, and it departed from platform 12. As I waited, I began to think and realise that all these young men on platform 12 going through the gate with suitcases must surely be headed for the same place. I found that comforting as I thought that I could simply become the grey man when we arrived at the Army training camp, I could simply coast my way through training as there would be to many of us to focus on any one individual; I soon learned how wrong that assumption was to be.

I asked one lad nearby where he was headed and he told me he was joining the Para's, the train arrived at Brookwood station and it was as though I was going backwards now, the station was even older than Great Yarmouth, and it seemed to be in the middle of nowhere.

However, I had arrived.

Chapter II

The Depot, day one

I remember the sun was shining very brightly and with a high heat that day and I wanted to take my suit Jacket off. However, I felt so smart and was so proud of it that I kept it on. Outside Brookwood station there is quite a large car park to the front and to the left is an even bigger one. In the bigger car park to the left there must have been around 15 to 25 young men like me just waiting, smoking, and chatting.

I joined them and waited for the transport to come and pick us up. There was a bus service listed in the joining instructions, but I did not even think about that as I knew I'd get lost. I asked a lad stood near me how long they had been waiting. He was from Wales and had been there since at least 09:30 AM like me he had set off very early it was now gone 10:30 by the time I had arrived.

Then came two minibuses and the two drivers were soldiers wearing black berets. I remember thinking that we would never all get in those two buses, and then one of them shouted, "Who is for Deepcut Barracks, Royal corps of transport, R.C.T?" to which about ten or so hands went up, and they made their way casually to the minibus. The RCT drivers, one with fag in hand said, "Welcome lads, it's not far, sorry it's a bit of a squeeze etcetera."

After what seemed an age, and two train loads of new recruits later, the same two minibuses with smoking drivers arrived and the entire process was repeated. I asked one of the drivers when the minibus was coming for the Guards depot, to which he just laughed and drove off!

At about 11:00, a Landrover and 4 tonne truck arrived in the front car park of Brookwood station, from the front passenger seat of the landrover stepped out what I can only describe as the tallest and smartest looking soldier I had ever seen. What is more, I recognised him to be a Coldstreamer from the white band on his cap!

He was a Lance sergeant, L/Sgt; therefore, he had two rows of crescent shaped brass bands glistening in the sun on the peak of his slashed forage cap. A forage cap is like a postman's or bus drivers cap, but the peak is cut or slashed and straightened to vertical with the tip of the bottom of the peak resting slightly over the eyebrows and at the bridge of the nose. It is a style mostly exclusive to the Guards and is very smart. He looked very tall and in number two dress, this is the khaki trousers and jacket worn for non-ceremonial parades.

I would come to know this L/Sgt very well as he was an instructor for my platoon for the next twelve months; his name was CM or Mal if you dared. He strode to the centre of the front car park and shouted for all those going to the Guards depot to move towards him, where he then asked how many out of the 15 or 20 or so assembled of us had been in the cadets of any kind? About 7, including me, raised our arms and we were told to go to the right and get into three ranks which we did with a small amount of fussing. He then told the rest to fall in alongside of us then told to pick up all our luggage, and pass it into the back of the four-tonne truck and get in.

I was confused and still waiting for the minibus to arrive, he then pointed to the PTI from the 4 Tonne truck passenger seat. I now know he was a PTI, or physical training instructor, as they wear distinctive tight-fitting navy-blue sleeveless tops, with burgundy red piping. The L/Sgt, said the drivers and PTI were there to aid him and that we were going to the Depot, which was about a mile away. Instructions were that we were not to smoke, lean out the back and to be silent the PTI being seated in the back with us.

We arrived at the entrance to the Guards depot, as we exited the truck a big white sign was there welcoming us. We were ushered into a nearby car park across the road from the Guards Depot Guard room behind the sentry box from which the barrier across the road was lifted and lowered. The PTI returned from the guardroom with a clip board and pen and as we assembled back into three ranks our names and dates of birth were taken.

It was then explained that we were going to be documented and processed, moreover a medical check carried etc, we were lined up facing the tree lined direction of the interior of the camp, and the following briefing was given, we were going to run, as no one walked in the depot either march or run, the PTI would be running with us to the processing place which I now know as the education / training centre. We were warned that this PTI was going to be setting the pace and if when we eventually stopped by another barrier in the camp, if you were behind him, you would be simply turned around and escorted back to the Guardroom as that person would not be wanted. Moreover, a rail warrant would be prepared out for that person to be used at Brookwood station for their return home!

It was now that I understood why that RCT driver laughed when he drove off,

"Turn to the left, and double Maaaarch!" L/Sgt CM shouted and off we trotted obediently.

At our School when doing country runs, I would hide in an old barn and have a fag with my then school friend Martin Dukes, we found the perfect place to look through an old broken slate in the roof so that we could see the class on the return leg, then re-join them but not sweating as they would pass by. That laziness now came back to haunt me as, after about only 100 meters or so my legs were like jelly, the case felt like it weighed a ton and all you could hear was the dismounted driver shouting very loudly to the PTI phrases like, "one gone." As the shouts reached the front PTI, I realised that this was people quitting and walking behind us trying to catch up. In the periodical times we walked it gave a chance for those to catch up, on the left-hand pavement I could see suitcases and bags being thrown onto it and collected by the supporting lorry and landrover driver. It was more like the Grand National, but we were the poor bloody horses jumping and dodging bags and cases rather than fences and ditches.

I was horrified and wanted to stop and simply walk. This was not how I had imagined it to be when I was in the Army cadets, which was midnight pillow fights, coco, and chocolate biscuits. I wanted to stop so desperately because my case felt like I was carrying two sacks of my old man's spuds instead to a customer helping him on his delivery round. Mum and the old man's words came back to taunt me,

"Daunt wurrey bout it iffun you dunt loik et our Garrrry, cum hum and do sumin else ats nou shame".

("Don't worry about it if you don't like it our Gary, come home and do something else there's no shame in that".)

We eventually turned right into a road lined with Yellow painted huts a Scottish soldier was playing a set of bag pipes on the veranda of the first wooden building on our right. I remember thinking how odd? Half way along this road I caught a glimpse of recruit guardsmen sweeping roads and other activities, I was so tired it was so tempting to stop bend over and get my breath as the sweat started stinging my eyes It would be so easy to just simply stop, but then I would look ahead and see the cut off PTI slightly ahead of me and try to muster the energy to keep going.

When the front group stopped occasionally to walk, I'd keep running and get back into the main throng of the group. I thought if I stayed ahead of him, the cut off PTI I would be all right. It was a mental conflict between Mum's words and keeping up with the cut off PTI. It did not help having that great big knot tied in the crotch of my underpants which was now really stressing me out.

How easy it would be to just stop, it was agonising, then....., then, it happened; some call it second breath, others call it adrenaline, but he was there, there in my mind's eye, JACK ! , Jack, with his saliva creamy cornered mouth waiting with his cane, stating again to my sweat saturated brain that I was a no good, and I'd be back in a week, at this rate I'd be back the same bloody day!

With that adrenaline infused rush, before I knew it, I was ahead of the "return home" PTI as we turned around at the crossroads near what I now know to be the Cinema and headed back in the direction we had come. I could see the young men still headed inwards to the camp who unless they really had extra in the tank were not going to make it. We turned left by the wooden hut headed in the direction we come from several of the Pipers had come to the veranda to watch us with wry smiles on their face as we chugged on by, eventually we started to walk again just before turning left into the centre of the depot.

As I was taking advantage of the walking to get my breath back, drawing in great gulps of oxygen from the Indian sub-continent, a white minibus passed by us. I recognised the driver to be that from the RCT recruits pick up earlier, I suppose heading back to Brookwood station to ferry other newly arrived recruits to Deepcut Barracks which I learned later they could use the main road in the depot as a short cut. It was then I heard my first Guardsman's term for any soldier not "blue, red, blue" the joint Guards insignia colours, "Chippie" whom I was told by a PTI not to look at because they were "Chippies"?

We started running again and turned left at a mini roundabout, I could see a white hut like that at the main entrance again in the near distance with a barrier across both sides of the road, the barrier was put up to allow us to pass through, the security barrier of my new home for the next twelve months. The barrier was put down after I had gone through. I joined on the grass bank the mass of coughing and wheezing young men whose cases had been thrown to the floor, PTIs shouting for them to "get up, stand up." I was in that number thank God.

I looked back to see the Landover slowly being driven towards us along the road from whence we had come, visibly bulging with bags and suitcase. After the Landrover had come across the barrier and parked on the left in front of the barrier the assembled mass, myself included were told to retrieve cases from the landrover, those who had not ditched theirs to pick up our case. I could clearly see those who had not been ahead of the return home PTI being ushered into a small group. I felt sorry for them. I never really found out if they were sent home or not, all I do know is that they were not with us as we walked the short distance to the processing centre. As we were getting into three ranks to do so I asked the PTI who told me not to look at the Minibus driver a little while ago what a chippie was?

In round about terms, it was explained to me that we, the Guards were a steak dinner with fine wine and classical music, the rest of the Army was Fish, N, Chips with a can of cheap pop and radio one, hence "Chippies".

It was quite amusing for me that almost 45 years after the events I am recalling that I heard my own son Martin, who also joined the Coldstream guards 30 years later use the term in conversation with me when referring to the staff at base camps and other regiments patrolling in other areas of operations in Afghanistan.

On reflection, this expectation on Guardsman to be better goes way back, an example I can cite, one of many, some years ago I read in a book about the WW1 exploits of Lt I.L. Read, Leicester's.

In the opening of the book, he recounts a meeting with a stranger who had passed by his house which he had named Berle`s after a village in France emblazoned in a WW1 battle many years before, the stranger realising the area was named after a battle torn village and had also served in WW1 asks him,

"What were you in? "Leicester's, we took over from the French and were there, [Berle`s] all the winter of 1915 I was hit in Monchy. What were you in? "He replied, "Coldstream Guards" we both laughed, and I said apologetically, 'Ah real soldiers!'

The medical centre as I came to know it was not where we all went for medicals and documentation processing, this was done in the training centre which could accommodate the fifteen or so of us in need of processing. We were all lined up in a very long central corridor with the shiniest floor I had seen in my life which squeaked as you walked upon it, we were counted off into smaller groups and were told we would have to follow the instructions given to us by a Lance Corporal, a Corporal being put in charge of each group. In my group we had an overly broad accented Scotsman dressed in green trousers known as barrack dress, shirt, tie, jumper, Brigade belt and highly polished black shoes known as barrack dress shoes. This ensemble was known collectively as barrack dress order.

My group entered a room where we were told to put our cases in the corner and get in two ranks, two files and undressed to underpants pants and socks, and be quiet about it.

My heart sank lower than the Titanic, surely not, please God no, this is not real.

After dithering I got down to my bare chest and left my trousers on, to which the Scots Guards Corporal looked up at me from his clip board and asked,

"What's the problem laddie?"

I ignored him and pretended not to hear, to which he repeated the question, again.

And again, I pretended not to hear him and continued to look at a picture of a machine gun stripped down into many parts on a poster on the facing wall.

He then took three quick steps towards me, and asked again whether I had a problem?

"Was I embarrassed ed to undress in front of the rest of the squad?" as he called us, more rapid-fire questions rising in tempo,
"Did I want a private room"?
"Was I worried about my Willie showing?
"Had mummy told me never to take my trousers off in front of strangers?"

23

The latter two Questions generating a giggle and muted laughter in the other ranks.

"No" I replied sheepishly".
"Then get your shagging trousers of like the rest".

He walked back to his spot and continued to ask all assembled their first and last names.
After several minutes he looked at me and stood dumb struck mouth open, after what seemed an age he finally, exclaimed,

"What on Gods good earth have we here?
"Get out here you, what are you fucking wearing laddie?"

I chose not to answer,

"Do you piss yer sen laddie? Turn around"

I held back,

"Are you fucking deaf as well as fucking stupid? "Turn around and face the squad".

I did so and could see the assembled red faced and busting not to laugh. He then addressed the squad.

"I ask you lot, I may be an old Scottish bastard with no sense of fashion, but please tell me these are not all the rage?"

Pointing at my knotted oversized pants with his clip board, he then said,

"Turn this way and face me son".

as I did the pants fell to the floor.

The whole room inclusive of admin staff, medics, and Doctor all now stood laughing hysterically as I bent down as fast as I could to pull them back up, this was exceedingly difficult to do as there was so much material to gather, with a loud shout and a very red face the Corporal told everyone to be quiet, he then asked me my name and in my very broad Norfolk dialect I replied,

"Moi name is Gaaarry Fish, coooorporul."

That was it, he started to laugh un-controllably, and with no need for prompting everyone else started laughing again.

This laughter coming from the room must have been audible from other rooms in the adjoining training offices, the Corporal quickly stifling his laughter when a tall uniformed senior rank with several civilian staff came into the room to see what was going on.

After repeated loud shouts of "Quiet!", the tall senior rank asked what was going on and the Corporal who was standing rigidly to attention pointed again with his clip board at my lower regions, the senior ranking Officer looked down in a very serious voice and said,

"Fuck me we are blessed, we have Mahatma Gandhi on parade, get the corps of drums out!"

Again, the whole room including associated staff and newly joined voyeurs of my predicament started to join in.

I had to justify myself, this was not my fault, after the laughter died down, I explained to the senior ranking Officer,

"Het hent moi fault lukeer, hets moi mums, her gern un brought me seconds from Yarrrmouth Maaarkut, hen there to big lukeer."

25

("It's not my fault look here, it was my Mum, she bought me these second-hand from Yarmouth Market and they're too big look.")

This only accentuated the laughter to another crescendo. The senior rank came over and asked me if I had flown all the way from Australia in these pants? To which I replied,

"Thas not rioght, oi hent a Australon , as that a jouk? I am from Norfolk, Great Yarrrmouth, near Narridge an Lowestaarft".

("That's not right, I am not an Australian is that a joke. I'm from Norfolk, Great Yarmouth, near Norwich and Lowestoft.")

More howls of laughter and the senior rank telling me it did not matter, but I could not walk around in these pants if they kept falling and told me to follow him. As I walked out of the room more laughter as the large knot tied at the crutch started to swing backwards and forwards between my lower legs just below the knees with each step.

He took me to a store where the store man gave me some green army string and I tied this around the waist of my pants and headed back down the corridor to re-join the rest of my squad.

After giving blood, being given various unknown injections, having to bend over and show your bum hole to the doctor by pulling the cheeks of your bum apart, this after he has just had a grip on your testicles whilst demanding a cough! For my fellow recruits this was an embarrassing time but for me it mattered not as I had more than my share of shame and embarrassment in the last hour with the untying and re tying of my nappy pants.

After re-dressing, we were moved into the next room and had to confirm our personal details. Once again, my address proved more cause for amusement coupled with my broad Norfolk accent, you see I lived in The Villa, The Street, Hemsby, Norfolk. The clerk asking me several times if I could repeat and was I sure, to which I would answer "of cause", he called over another clerk in uniform and asked me to repeat, I did so and he chuckled and said to the clerk dealing with me, "You've a right Norfolk dumpling there, house and street names a bit complicated!"

I was given my eight-digit army number on a printout and told not to lose it. I looked at it and it also said Grenadier Guards! I imagine that if any ex-Coldstreamers are reading this they will realise what an affront that is. I remonstrated with the clerk and explained I was supposed to be in the Coldstream, but he would not budge on the matter, so was moved along. When I got outside the office, I spotted a Coldstream guards Corporal in the corridor and went to complain to him. I came to know him very well his name was MG, he would be my barrack room instructor for the next twelve months, a barrack room instructor lives with you in the room in a 'bunk', a bunk is a separate small en-suite room to the main barrack room. His job is to teach you all you need to know about cleaning kit, and other necessities of becoming a Guardsman.

I explained to him that I had joined the Coldstream as my Granddad had been in them. He wasted no time and after telling me to wait went away and brought a senior with him, also wearing a Coldstream forage cap, and before I knew it, I was back in the office and the error was quickly corrected with lots of banter between him and the Corporal from the Grenadiers, Corporal MG pretending to spit on the floor saying bloody gobblers nice try?

Two members of Gibraltar two waiting to be processed I do not think I was in that group.

Corporal MG asked if there were any others. Meaning new Coldstream recruits? After checking up there was not, he asked me to pick up my things and follow him. When we got outside, he explained that you did not walk in the depot, particularly past what he called the Kremlin, and pointed up the road to a small brick-built office block facing the short end of the square. I asked him why this was called the Kremlin and he explained it was where all the high-ranking people work the Depot Regimental sergeant major R.S.M. the Commandant, he said if you could not march you ran, he took of my suit jacket and showed me where we were going to run to and off, we went at a gentle pace him alongside me along what's called Adair walk.

Adair walk runs along the length of the huge drill square and after getting about halfway down an officer was walking up towards us and he told me to stand still. He sprung to attention by what is known as pulling your feet in, he threw up a smart salute and the officer said thank you and to carry on.

We then continued at a steady pace towards my destination Marlborough block opposite the Gym. He took me up to the second floor and told me this was my room and to take any bed I liked as I was only the second person there. I asked him to do that salute again and I could see he was a bit flustered by my request and said there would be time enough for that and left.

After he had gone, I heard the toilet flush and from the ablutions as I came took now it, out of there came a very tall well-built young man with golden blonde hair, the type of person Adolf Hitler would have been proud to suggest as the perfect "Ayrian" on posters during WWII.

He walked to the middle of the room and gestured his hand, which I took and shook, he told me his name was RA from Truro in Cornwall. I laughed and he looked puzzled as to why. I pointed out we were both wearing that same Burtons suit, he looked and started to laugh as well, I said, "£50.00 on sale Burtons Great Yarmouth market two days ago" he said £45:00 on sale Burton Truro last week!" He asked if I was from the isle of Wight.

I explained that it was Great Yarmouth Norfolk, RA had already made his bed and I asked him where he got his sheets. He told me that due to the length of the journey from Cornwall he had travelled the day before and had arrived late last night. He showed me where the bedding was in my 'top locker' and that Corporal MG had told him we must use the mattress cover and showed me what that was. He showed me where Corporal MG`s room was, and I made my bed while I had a good look around the room. The room was square in the middle and on one wall was a shelf with a TV Ariel and plug socket and the opposing wall had a large, framed picture on with many faces of men from various times in history all Coldstream Victoria Cross winners, each contained a small citation of what they had done to win the medal and where.

On the periphery of the room were small enclaves and each had three beds within it as shown in the appendix. I had the view out through the small window which opened by sliding the bottom half of the window to the top, below was another platoon room with an identical layout to ours. In this room, RA told me, were soldiers in training just like us but they had been there for quite a while, he had seen them that morning go off on training.

It was now about 2 o'clock and up until now I had not felt hungry but when I opened my suitcase I had forgotten about my sandwiches of cheese and tomato wrapped in a Sainsbury bag. I offered half to RA, but he had already eaten so I went to the table and, as I chatted to RA, I found we had much in common. We were both from a seaside town and had spent the last couple of years working rides and chasing after holiday making girls.

During the afternoon, increasingly new recruits were being brought to the room by Corporal MG. They came in twos and threes all day, I was approached by a northern lad called SR who was from Newcastle, he offered his hand and said his name, Corporal MG overheard and told not just me but all those present we were not to use our first names with each other but surnames only. I found this a bit odd but who were we to argue, in any case I had absolutely no idea what he was asking me, he said, "how man, hev yee gorra tab marror please?" I had no idea what he was on about other than noticing the word marrow? I explained I had eaten my sandwiches and had none left. SR became frustrated and spoke slower this time asking the same question but gesturing with two fingers to his mouth.

I still shrugged my shoulders as I had no idea what he was trying to tell me. I felt like I was in a scene with Lassie' i.e., trying to understand the barking of a cleverer than average dog and its meaning that someone somewhere was in trouble. After repeating the question to me for a third time, I began to get worried as I thought what he wanted was a fight! He was becoming very frustrated but luckily Corporal MG stepped in and translated that he wanted a cigarette to which I obliged while still confused if that is what he really wanted, or if he was just pleased to get a free cigarette.

The room was getting quite full, it held 24 beds divided into three beds in eight enclaves. I was asked by BG if the bed next to mine was taken when he arrived, which it was not, and he started to unpack after I had given him the same advice about mattress cover etc I had received from

31

RA. He was from Essex, and I was relieved as I understood every word he was saying. I asked Corporal MG on one of his trips to the room bringing in new recruits if there was a phone and he said there was at the NAFFI and that he would show me it after "scoff". Again, I had no idea what that meant but at least I knew there was a phone.

By mid-afternoon the room was almost full, and another chap called SO took the third bed in our enclave, he was from the Birmingham or the Coventry area. What was noticeable was that he had large buck teeth.

At teatime Corporal MG explained that we all needed to wash our hands and make sure we used a nail brush as he was going to take us all to "Scoff". Someone, I forget who, asked him what scoff was and he explained it was food, meals from breakfast to dinner or any meal. Still confused I asked again why Scoff? and he patiently explained further that you did not take your time at meals you scoffed it down as quick as you can. He also explained that in the depot you marched or ran as an individual or as a group to meals with berets on and waist belt worn, however, after eating you walked smartly back in an easy break step with no beret and belt. However, as we could not march at present, we would all run I was getting a bit fed up with this no walking and running business, someone asked what time Scoff would be and the answer again confusingly given by Corporal MG was when it was blown or around 17:30 hrs. I was not the only one I am sure that neither understood what blown meant or 17:30hrs for that matter.

It was a gradual process, but the room was almost full and in each enclave conversations and new friendships were being formed and then a trumpet was sounded quite a distance off, and we all wondered what it was. Corporal MG told us Scoff was now on and checked whether we had all cleaned our hands? All agreed and we went downstairs and after a rough three ranks were formed, we all jogged together in what shortly did not resemble three ranks any longer. Corporal MG's frustration was obvious, I am not now, and especially back then ever been a body language expert, but I could see he was very red in the face and biting his bottom lip by the time we arrived at the cook house. It was made worse I noticed when someone called out to him when we heard the trumpet again "What's that trumpet for Corp?" He remonstrated with that person after finding out he was an ex-Army cadet and I realised that it was not wise to admit I had been a cadet also from the expression he gave the guy after being called that. He did go on to explain that it was not a Trumpet but a Bugle and that all meals and other orders such as revile, fire, lights out, last post was announced by Bugle played by a Drummer and that all the calls would be explained later. I was beginning to wonder what Army I was in; I was sure that was from my Granddads' time.

We queued up with at least a hundred other new recruits in civilian clothing all chatting away when an officer and a Sergeant came out through the door in no two dress , without warning and very loudly Corporal MG shouts Shut Up !, Standstill ! , which due to the level and violence in the voice we all did, he then took a short step forward with his left foot and right arm hand making a fist and as quick as a flash brought the leg backwards and next to his right, and then bent his right leg thigh parallel to the ground stamped it down hard and saluted, he then dropped his right arm and asked, "May I have you Permission to carry on sir please?" to which the officer replied at the same time as saluting, "yes please" Corporal MG re saluted dropped his right arm turned slight to his right and again raised his right knee thigh parallel to the ground and stamped his right leg and foot back down again making a thud as it hit the floor, and then shouted carry on to all of us, but no one said anything I think Like me they were a bit stunned at what that was about?

The queue went down very quickly and when I got nearer to the door, I could see through a window why, the inside was massive with a long serving point with many white hat wearing chefs ladling out the food. However, before you got in you had to show your hands to an NCO, the NCSO at the door were very young looking and I found out later that they were training recruits the same as us but had rank with a red backing around the chevrons' they were called junior NCO and chevrons are what the Guards call "Stripes" it's the chippie mobs that call them stripes. Corporal MG had to override the Junior NCSO from sending some recruits away to re wash their hands as some still had dirt under the fingernails, I was ok and passed through, but I did see Corporal MG with slightly raised voice explain to those stopped about "Dirty Flesh".

Dirty flesh could result in a bath being prepared by your peer group and all sorts of cleaning products being used by the remainder of the squad taking turns scrubbing you clean with yard brushes etc. If your shirt collar and cuffs had tide marks on them even though they had been washed could be deemed as dirty flesh. At one time OS accused RA of wearing his underpants which of course he had not. The reason was we had to use a common drying room to launder and dry our clothes, RA in an act of vengeance when OS was not looking RA took his underpants from his locker and put brown boot polish in the gusset no matter how hard OS scrubbed that brown staining it would not come out and he spent the next few weeks and at every room and locker inspection sweating they would not be found, much to the amusement of all of us in on the prank.

I was absolutely amazed by the choice of food available joints of meat, and it was not Sunday, we only had chicken on Sunday at home other than that it was egg, beans, or something on toast! I was dithering at the choices and the chefs were rather gruff asking "come on what do you want, hurry up we haven't got all day" I could see further down the line that the long serving point actually ran from two directions and that speeded things up, I could also see ahead of me that the chefs measured everything three potatoes, if four were on the ladle one was tipped back into the tray and the vegetables were levelled in the spoon, I sat down in a space on one of the very long tables RA sat next to me and asked why I had no pudding ? I explained that I never really ate puddings, I just liked my diner and he asked if I could get one and give mine to him which I agreed I went back up saying I had forgotten to get my pudding, on my return RA asked me again to confirm I never ate pudding and he smiled as I confirmed not, I think from his smile I had found a permanent dining partner! RA was by far the tallest in our room, he was at least 6ft 5inches tall and very well built, and I soon learned that RA was always hungry.

After tea or "Scoff" we went back to the room walking but in silence as Corporal MG walked just behind us telling us to turn left here and right there, we were quite lucky as our block was not that far from the Cook house, as we moved along Corporal MG would tell us what each building was, the barbers etc, and he explained we would get the grand tour soon of the whole camp.

When we arrived back outside the block another Corporal whom I came took now as Corporal HC, who was the other barrack room instructor for the other 24 man room across the corridor from us; he had about 10 or so new recruits with him and he asked Corporal MG how he was and how big the queue was, someone I forget who but a new recruit pitched in and said it's not that long, I saw now as did some others that Corporal MG and Corporal HC were different people as Corporal HC tore into him, " Don't ever but into my conversations again you little shit or I will bounce you from here to your next birthday, do you understand ? "To which a sheepish reply was given "yes" Corporal MG was smiling and I think he had been dying to do that all day...

I asked Corporal MG if I could go back the way we had come as he had pointed out the NAAFI, en-route back from Scoff, the NAAFI is a type of club / shop and had the three wooden panelled phone cubicles in it. The shop sold everything from cigarettes to shoe polish as we all soon learned at a vastly exaggerated price compared to Civilian Street. He agreed as he remembered I had asked earlier and he warned me to make sure I jogged his memory, I explained that actually I could march, I then remembered the cadets issue when asked how I explained that my granddad had been a Coldstreamer, he remembered from the Orderly room or clerk's office from earlier in the day, I explained that my Granddad had been teaching me for some weeks before coming to the depot, he watched me as I marched away and I heard nothing so kept going.

At the phone box, I dialled home to Norfolk and as my mother picked up the phone, before she had chance to ask who it was, I desperately blurted out,

"I need pants! I need new pants!"

My mother was I think a bit taken a back and after confirming.

"Is that you our Garrrrry?"

She asked me what was wrong had I been mugged for my new pants? before I got chance to answer she put her hand over the phone, I could hear her muffled explanation to the rest of the house,

"It's our Garrrrry he has been mugged and they have stolen his new pants".

frustrated I waited for her to stop panicking and the old man came on the phone to confirm whether Id had my best new pants stolen? I replied,

"No, I just need new pants as the ones I had were far to big".

The old man, repeated this to my mother but she would not believe me and was convinced that my pants had been stolen and asked the old man to find out what else had been taken? I said again in a loud voice that no! my pants had not been stolen but I needed new ones, after a while.

I was believed, and the old man told me that the vicar was here and that they had all been waiting for me to call and why had I waited so long to call? I now realised why my mother was in such as state and I felt a bit guilty at not calling sooner, the important question now was where to send smaller pants to and of course I had no idea!

After leaving my mum reassured, I would call again with the address I hung up and left the booth to sniggers from those in the queue waiting to use the not so private public phones, would these dreadful underpants never stop embarrassing me? Back at the room I became aware that the room was now full and indeed into the area in the middle extra beds were being set up to accommodate the extra people who had arrived and the same was happening across in Corporal HC room as I was asked to help carry the empty beds and mattress from the room below ours.

The recruits below us had returned from training and eyed us new recruits with slight mocking as we carried the beds from their room to our floor. It was about 7pm when we were all told to sit on our beds by Corporal MG and get a pen, paper and envelope; he then told us to get out our cards containing our numbers and write a short note to our next of kin stating this is my Address , 24513644 Junior Guardsman Fish, Coldstream guards, Gibraltar II L/Sgt HK squad, Guards Depot Surrey, he then told everyone to seal the envelope and if needed buy a stamp from him, we handed this to him as he was going to post them en-massed.

He also explained that we must start to remember the number given as it would not be accepted not to have memorised it by the end of the week and today was a Tuesday and that only gave us three days, it is odd now thinking back how that caused me such anxiety as I thought I would never remember it and I think I could recite that number with my dying breath now.

After all the kafuffle of handing in the letters was over Corporal MG came out to the middle of the room and shouted, "who the fuck is TM and Fish?" after a short pause I put my hand up and so did another youth in a large trench coat with big ears, Corporal MG asking us both if we were related?

To which in unison we shook our heads, he then asked again are we sure? Again a bemused head shaking and then he exclaimed that we must be as we must have both come from the same imbecilic parents as we had both addressed our envelopes to ourselves at the depot and not our families this was met with tumultuous roars of laughter from the room and Corporal MG asking if we would like to stay near each other in the same enclave as he preferred to have all the mongs in one place, I explained I had unpacked and he simply went back to his bunk after un ceremoniously chucked our letters back into the room, I re opened mine and re addressed ed it correctly and took it to Corporal MG's bunk for posting, he took it and said I can see we are going to have fun and games with you.

At about 8 pm a stocky moustached man came into the room wearing a tracksuit and carrying a very highly polished pair of black boots, a man accompanied him slightly taller also spouting a moustache and wearing a track suit, he in turn was followed by the very tall Sergeant and a L/Sgt CM I had seen at the station earlier that day. They all headed into Corporal MG's room and after a few minutes Corporal MG told us all to get into the middle of the room, Corporal HC brought all those from his room and was accompanied by yet another moustached man in tracksuit, we were all told to stop "chuntering" another expression meaning to shut up, we should stop talking.

The table from the middle of the room was moved to the wall and on top of it climbed Sgt R McM who introduced himself as the Platoon sergeant of Gibraltar II. He then went on to explain that although the rooms were overflowing with many beds that situation would change soon, and he apologised for the squashed conditions, I thought for a moment about empty beds in the room below the platoon were called Flanders II, was their room once this packed? In any case, he went on to introduce in turn each instructor as they stood on a chair so we could see them, first the man in the tracksuit carrying boots was L/Sgt HK , I should mention that a Lance Sergeant rank is abbreviated as L/Sgt and the rank is particular to the Guards in pay terms it is actually a Corporal rank who normally wear two chevrons' in the chippie mobs, but due to Queen Victoria wanting her Guards NCSO to be held above the others decreed that they would have three chevrons' instead of the two normally worn by Corporals or Cpls and that they should be called L/Sgts.

It was L/Sgt HK who would be our drill instructor in this room, next he introduced the person who followed him in in his name was L/Sgt CM, he was the drill instructor for the other room looked after by Corporal HC, the next person introduced was the one who followed Corporal HC in and he was introduced as L/Sgt TC who would be the weapons and tactics instructor for the room next door. Sgt R McM explained that another L/Sgt was also joining us for the weapons and tactics training called L/Sgt TB he was unable to come along this evening and lastly that we would meet the platoon commander Lt D at the right time. He then went onto explain that the year ahead would be tough and challenging and that we could rest assured we would not make it through the year if we did not work hard and try, he was not after expert soldiers who could do anything straight away but rather thought more of those who never gave in and kept trying and guaranteed that was the way ahead.

He gave another reason for why it was going to be tough it would be difficult to make the grade the reason given was that all the instructors had good reputations back in the Battalions they had come from, and that if they allowed sloppy standards to get through it reflected bad on them lastly, he stated that we were now potential Guardsmen, and that to remove the word Junior from our current rank to simply Guardsman serving in a Battalion and to wear the bearskin cap was a privilege to be bought at great cost from Guardsman who had gone before us and they would expect nothing less , he then gestured to the wall upon which the 13 Victoria Cross winners were displayed from the Coldstream guards history and battles, he was confident we would know more about them than our own parents by the time we had been here 8 weeks then

L/Sgt HK called out in a very loud shout "Room!" and Corporal MG and Holman stood to attention and we instinctively knew to be quite as Sgt R McM left the room L/Sgt HK shouted, "May I have your Permission to carry on Sgt Please?" to which came the reply "carry on L/Sgt HK".

All the recruits under Corporal HC were shuffled back to their room and we left in our room were told to get into three or four ranks in front of the table and L/Sgt HK stood on the table and explained that from tomorrow we would be starting drill and admin and that we needed to understand the basic things going on here, he explained that when any rank walked into the room the first person to see them was to announce to the room by shouting "Room,"! It was then that no matter what you were doing you had to spring to attention as the reporter and the rest to do likewise that would be sufficient for us to understand and that Corporal HC will teach us these basic things and to learn well as not understanding was not acceptable. It was then that I heard it for the first time, the threat, he explained that as un-employment was running rife, and that the Army had just been given the best pay rise ever by the new Conservative Thatcher government the army was oversubscribing and that he could afford to lose many of us as there were plenty of young men joining up far more than in the previous decade. He would personally ensure that at the end of every day training he would have a rail warrant ready to send us home on the train if any one of us was being idle on drill or any Less on for that matter. It was a scary statement and I thought back to my first thoughts in Waterloo station on seeing all those new recruits there and at Brookwood that I would be able to just coast my way through training like I did at School. No Chance.

He then left and Corporal MG told us that everyone must take a shower before bed and that lights out would be at 22:00hrs i.e., 10 pm. I then faced that situation again with my pants; I went to the ablutions or toilet shower and bath area and to my relief a lockable bath, sanctuary! I could undress and get my pyjamas on with no shame, I had never worn pyjamas before, but they were on the packing list, so Mum had bought some for me. The room did have an air of excitement about it after the instructors had left and about a quarter to ten I went to the bathroom to change and have a bath, when I emerged from the bathroom everyone had been to the shower and the main lights were out, everyone had their small bedside lights on which were situated above the head board and were of a low wattage and subsequently quite dim, however, I could still be seen by Corporal MG sitting at the table now repositioned into the middle of the room who started laughing at me and asked if I seriously wore pyjamas ? I said I normally did not and that I slept at home in pants, he said I should do the same here and should change, my heart stopped, and Corporal MG asked in general, who else was wearing pyjamas? No one was, and I think he asked this to show me I was not alone; however, one Geordie lad came out of the shower stark naked and jumped into bed, Corporal MG asked him where his pants were and he replied,

"Ah divvint weor pants"

Corporal MG asked why? He replied,

"Ah divvint ahn any pants nivver have, except yen time
when me ma wes sick an' wuh weor leukt eftor by the
chorch the' made wor weor pants but me da tyeuk
them off wor an wair them himself when wuh went hyem agyn,"

Translate Geordie,

(I don't own any pants never have, except one time when, me ma was sick and we were looked after by the church, they made us wear pants, but my dad took them off me and wore them himself when we went home again)

This statement left Corporal MG in stitches and he explained he must wear pants in the army and that he would be Issued with some soon, I was also relieved to hear that and Corporal MG told us all lights out and that reveille would be at 07:30 hrs in the morning and Scoff would be at 08:30hrs, I asked BG if he knew what 07:30 hrs was and he said half past seven I thought that was quite reasonable as on camp with the cadet's it was normally six thirty, things were looking up it can't be all that bad. I tried to sleep but kept tossing and turning until well past midnight and then someone started crying in the room sobbing and another person got up at about 01:00hrs and went to Corporal MG's room asking to go home I was just too tired by now to listen to what was going on eventually,

I fell fast asleep the last thoughts I had were that the first day was over.

Chapter III

Barrack room instruction, the way of the Junior Guardsman

At 07:30hrs sharp I was awoken by Corporal MG shacking my foot and stating it was time to get up, he flicked on my bedside light which was located above my headboard and attached to the wall, it shone down wards towards the pillow. He was going around each bed space repeating the same thing, one by one we all woke up and sat in some cases like stunned slugs, he explained that no one was to go to the ablutions [Washroom] until he told us to and that we should get our washing and shaving kit out.

We all filed into the washroom and were told that we were going to be taught how to shave; Corporal MG asked who had already shaved themselves before and after establishing that most had not, he went onto demonstrate. The First thing we were told was that you never ever shaved with your shirt or vest on, that you would be considered a minger if you did so [again more un explained slang words] and someone equally as confused as me thankfully asked what a minger was? he explained that a minger was a dirty person, a person who would bring dirt and disease into the room and in the field , meaning when at war, he reminded us of the fact that we had previously shown our hands at scoff yesterday and that anyone found with dirty hands would be reported for what can be officially charged as "Dirty flesh" he went on that anyone not correctly shaved can also be charged and fined for having dirty flesh; so we should pay attention to what he was about to teach us.

He stripped to the waste and started by explaining that the water if available must be ran hot first until you could not put your hand underneath it, it must then be switched off and cold water started and only then add the hot water to it thereby saving on the hot water for everyone else, this he remarked may seem odd as we were in a washroom; but we should apply this principle as in the field we would have to wash from hot water if allowable and at times this may come from a Mess tin and a hot brew and a warm wash were achievable with hot water conservation. This did make sense.

He then took his razor and explained that you should if possible, shake the blade in the hot water first to attempt to sterilise it, and he did so, he then used a shaving stick and brush and made a lather from the stick onto a brush, he put this down and then put the clean hot water onto his face and stated this was to give the skin some moister before applying the brush which he then did.

He then took the razor and explained that you should find your own method but try to always repeat it each time you shave so that if you had to, you could shave without the aid of a mirror again in the field. He then shaved his face and after each pass with the blade he washed the razor in the sink; after he was finished shaving, he then washed his face in the lathery water and explained that to reduce weight in webbing or field kit this stick served as both soap and shaving cream, he then made a repeated statement in a very serious voice saying it twice, that we should make effort upon the neck and behind the ears.

He then asked if we had any questions many hands went up and the first to ask was SP, he was very fair skinned and although we all in retrospect looked our ages of 16, he looked more 12 or 13 years old he asked if he had to shave as he did not grow face hair! This caused a laugh and others stated the same, however, Corporal MG stated no exceptions all must shave, another question was then asked accompanied by several all-nodding heads in agreement that they did not own a razor. This was not an Issue for Corporal MG and he went to his bunk [A small one-man room just for him] and came back with a pack of yellow Bick razors and dished them out to those without blades, he asked those with shaving cream to share and that all should put these items a razor spare blades and shaving stick and brush onto their list of things needed when they went to the Navy, Army Air Force Institute shop, [NAAFI].

We all queued one behind the other watching and advising the man in front at the sink with the enthusiasm of the task like professional barbers in a shop. When the last man was finished Corporal MG went into the ablutions and with a loud exclamation shouted "what the fuck has happened in here?" he came rushing back out, and asked us all to gather into the centre of the room, he then looked at all our faces quizzing each one as he passed and then stopped at PS and as he looked we all looked and poor PS was bleeding all over his face and holding his towel to his face every now and then in an attempt to stem the bleeding, Corporal MG told him he was 'only supposed to shave the fine hairs off not the first layer of skin !' He asked another I forget who, to bring him to the washroom and hold his head under the cold shower to stop the bleeding, in addition a few others including myself were sent to clean the sinks. As I went in, I could hear PS protesting at the cold water I could also see why Corporal MG was alarmed a few moments ago it looked more like an abattoir that a washroom, every sink had blood in it, around it and on the floor, was awash with blood, we must have been a bit over enthusiastic in our task.

We were all told to parade outside at the front of the barrack block and in our threes again ran [doubled] to the cook house for breakfast or scoff, after showing hands we went in, and it was surprisingly quite compared to the evening before. I now know this was due to the fact that we had been awakened with all the other 'new draft' later than normal as a sort of breaking in gently I think... RA kept asking me if I wanted this or wanted that as I ate and I gave him my Cornflakes as again I do not eat those or as previously stated puddings, he was he agreed onto a good thing eating next to me, even so after he had finished he was still hungry and sat like a vulture scanning to see when anyone finished if they left anything and would politely ask 'could I have that?' and then if permission given promptly scoff down the leftover item of food! It was not that there was not enough to eat, just that RA was always hungry, the chefs at the depot did everything by the book and you got one sausage, one bacon slice, one egg fried or one level spoon of scrabbled etc.

I remember as we queued up that the younger chefs behind the hot plate who of course were the lowest form of chippie mob looked puzzled at Smith who was covered in bits of toilet paper and wandering what hellish thing had happed to him, they were attached to the depot and must have been aware of the harsh training happening all around them. What began to annoy all was the petty bullying that would happen at the hot point as time went on if you tried and RA did many times sneak a larger than normal ladle of scrambled eggs, potatoes etc that a chef would whack your knuckles with a ladle knowing full well he could get away with it after all we were the lowest form of life, 'new draft' 'sprogs' 'crows' as we eventually knew ourselves to be.

The food was very good but, on the walk back to the block a couple of lads were sick, I think it was due to eating fried food in the early morning and that most never ate breakfast, I know I certainly never did, and if I did it would only ever be a couple of slices of toast on weekends 'while watching the adventures of Robinson Crusoe or Belle and Sebastian, Wild horses and Flashing blades. After one of these stops to allow someone else to be sick Corporal MG explained that like shaving it was something we had better get used to as breakfast was compulsory it was a "Commandant's parade" the Commandant being the man in overall charge of everyone at the depot. If you missed breakfast, it was another chargeable offence.

I was becoming worried at all these charges and when we arrived back in the room, I asked Corporal MG where we would get the money for all these charges? He went bright red and told me to wait outside his bunk and went away coming back with Corporal HC and told me to repeat what I had just said to him, and so I did,

"Oi dunt understand et, where we ganna get enough money for all these charges Cpl.?

Corporal HC asking me what charges, and so I went further.

"For heven dirrrty flesh and missing breakfast?

He then twigged and started laughing and walked off wishing Corporal MG good luck with that one Corporal MG explained that charges were not financial charges they were Reports like having to see the principal when doing something wrong at School except military law was applied and you had a charge sheet listing your offence. He did though say I was partially correct and that if you were guilty of the charge levelled against you could get deductions from your pay as a punishment. I then said something stupid but at the time I meant it and said, I was not worried about pay as I was in the Army cause id always wanted to and I

48

was not bothered if they did not want to pay me! Corporal MG exploded into laughter and told me Maggie could do with a 100.000 more like me and walked off.

Corporal MG went around the room looking at the beds and asked us all who thought that the way we had made our beds was good enough for a Guardsman? needless to say, no one put their hands up and he explained that he was now going to teach us how to make our beds and that this would be expected from now on as a standard. He told us to move some of the overflow beds from the middle of the room and to put one bed in the middle where the table was and a bedside cabinet, as we were doing this at least two of the lads went to see him in his bunk after having had a muffled conversation in the corner and I was not the only one wondering what they were whispering about and when they came out from Corporal MG's room it became obvious as they started to pack up all there kit, they were leaving, they had had enough, I remember saying to BG blimey I didn't think breakfast was that bad ! To which he did laugh.

As we were clearing the space L/Sgt HK came into the room and no one shouted room and just carried on and that was the first time I saw him lose his temper after doing 25 press ups called out by him, he collected the three from Corporal MG and left, again we forgot to call Room! Ask permission to carry on and we were dealt another 25 press ups. We made the space and placed one of the beds into the middle of the room and placed a bedside locker next to it, Corporal MG then gathered us around the bed and locker in a half circle and held up and explained each piece of bedding starting with pillows x 2 Pillow case x 2 Blanket GS x 4 and he showed each of us the three red stripes that ran through the centre of the blanket the entire oblong side of the blanket and then exactly the same stripes in the two issued sheets, he then showed us the orange counterpane or what is also called the bed spread and lastly the mattress cover with three strings at the open end.

He explained that he was going to teach us how to make our beds each morning and what is known in the Army as a bedding block. He explained that each blanket and sheet must be folded and measure the same width and length and that if we got this wrong the bedding block would be rejected at the morning inspection which would be a daily occurrence, what rejected came to mean soon became clear over the next year.

The first step was to put the mattress cover on and to tie the draw strings together with three twists and have a singular bow knot and that the knot should be tucked inside the mattress cover bed springs side down with the open end of the cover facing the headboard, we all went away stripped our beds and did the same, I've come took now this type of training as monkey see, monkey do. We then were shown how to make the base or fit the counterpane, and this was done with what is known as hospital corners and the angle of the corner must run from the exact corner of the top of the mattress and be no wider that four fingers at the base when turned.

We had to establish the centre of the mattress and make a small mark with a pen on the metal bed frame where this was by halving the counterpane on the mattress before fitting it. Hurriedly we also went to do this, next we watched as Corporal MG placed a GS blanket onto the bedside locker and folded the blanket in such a way as the three red stripes ended up in the middle and he then placed this on the bed full length from head board to the bottom ready as he said to fill the remaining bedding into it, he then folded the next blanket in the same way using the bedside cabinet as a guide to the width and then he folded the blanket in on itself ending up with what resembled a pillow folded in half again the three red stripes were dead centre off the rolled blanked, he then placed this equidistant in the blanket on the bed and repeated the folding exactly the same way with a sheet and placed that on top of the preceding blanket and then another blanket on top of that followed by a sheet and finally the last blanket, it was similar to a lasagne! The three red strips were ensured as running in line with each other and the whole thing was wrapped around by the extended blanket making a kind self-containing box, the wrap around blanket had to have the last fold at the base and not on the top the bedding block had to be exactly in the centre, and this is where the three strips came in handy as they lined up with the previous pen mark.

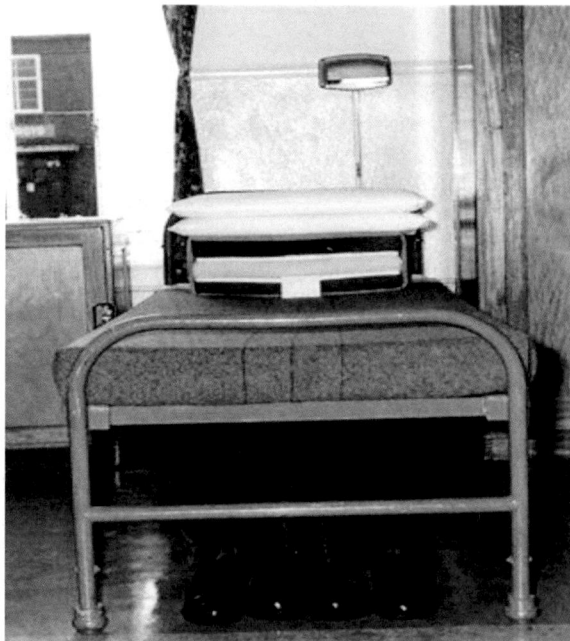

Bedding block and bed made down.

The pillows were placed into the cases and then folded to make further box shapes with no open ends showing and placed at the top resting against the headboard. Corporal MG stood back and explained the key thing was to use the bedside locker as a guide although it took longer it makes it easier and more exact.

He asked if anyone had any questions and SD his hand up, we were told we should not put our hands up as we were not at School, we should simply say yes Cpl, and so after being corrected SD asked, "when do we get to ride on tanks?" Corporal MG immediately blew his top and told us all to get outside, shouting get out, get out, get the fuck out! We all rushed as one jostling for space down the stairs as he was following us screaming his head off, I was actually a bit frightened, When we got outside on the road the window was opened from the platoon offices located between both rooms one of the Sergeants asked what was going on and Corporal MG replied that we had a comedian in the platoon and pointed SD out, the poor lad was asked by Corporal MG standing very close   to his face "did he think he was funny?" And I think SD in his Dorset accent very slowly replied or at least tried to explain that he was asking a question as Corporal MG had indeed asked if anyone had any questions after the bed block making lessons.

At this Corporal MG stood him in front of us all then turned us all around facing up the road towards the medical centre and pointed out a large bin in the distance and after confirming we could all see it told us he would send home that day the last man to touch that bin and get back into three ranks in front of him Go! off we all went at full pelt I was for one, very worried about being sent home and was running as fast as my legs could carry me and as we turned and headed back SD was still stood with Corporal MG, as we stood to attention couching and spluttering he asked SD who was last ? SD not wishing to cause any more trouble said he could not tell and so Go! was shouted again and off we all went like the clappers to that bin again and back, again the same question and again the same answer, Go! We were off again and upon our return this time Corporal MG asked SD if he had any funnier questions, and he replied No Cpl poor SD was almost in tears of frustration and Corporal MG called it a draw and we should all get back inside NOW! And off we went like lunatics rushing up the stairs back to the room.

It was about 10:00hrs and Corporal MG told us it was NAAFI break but as we were busy we would skip this and he explained that from 10:00 hrs to 10:30 hrs we had a mid-morning break but as we were now behind time due to silly bollocks pointing at SD we did not have time, he also informed us that each day someone had to take this steel bucket which was in the corner of the room and go to the kitchen and fill it with tea, however as we did not have cups yet this was pointless . He told SD he was duty tea Wallah for the next day if we had cups by then. In addition, we should add cups to our ever-increasing shopping list for pay day on next Thursday.

When we had finished making our bedding blocks Corporal MG asked to stand at the foot of our beds with the left or right knee in line with the bed corner dependent on the location of the bed, he then explained that whenever he shouted "Stand by Your Beds!" this is where as quickly as possible we should go to and he called us all into the middle of the room and then shouts "Stand by your beds" he then produced a long stick with a handle on it and called our attention to it and explained that it was his bedding block measuring stick and that he would have a look at our beds and show how this was used to measure the length and width, he then went around the room and held this length and breadth of our efforts and declared that it was not a bad effort and that we should pick the bedding blocks up and unravel them and that we should note that we were allowed no more than five minutes to make these in the morning after we got up and so when he said go we had to make them again as fast as we could with him timing us, we spent the next hour making and un making these bloody bedding blocks with Corporal MG timing them it was reminiscent of some scene in Nelsons navy drilling the gun crews in reloading cannon expect we were folding sheets and blankets.

We were all paraded outside and walked in threes by Corporal HC to Scoff, I was feeling full of breakfast, and it only seemed like five minutes from that meal to this and as usual the long queues were mind numbing and after scoff, we had been told to look forward to hair cutting.

We paraded and doubled to the barbers and as only three chairs were available at a time the rest of us not getting a haircut were taken outside by Corporal MG and we practiced standing at ease and bracing up our bodies, then falling into three ranks quickly from a rabble, this went on between shouts of 'next!' and as each file went in with long hair typically associated with the late 1970s they came out with a very, very short back and sides, when it came my turn I remember being confused as you went in the person next getting a haircut left his seat and the person swinging the floor bumper stopped took that seat and handed over the task to you.

A hand polishing bumper is a very heavy metal square shaped lump the size of a standard shoe box, it had a long wooden handle and attached to the bumper by a pin which swivelled through an arched fulcrum, on its base and in contact with the linoleum floor were short stubby bristles which when swung backwards and forwards in a pendulum motion by the user polished the floor, it was bloody hard work as the floor was thick with hard wax which smelt to me a bit like Vaseline.

A Bumper

I took over the bumper without needing instruction as I had seen what the last lad had been doing when I went into the barbers in a few minutes I was working up a sweat, and then Next was shouted and the next person came in and looked at what I was doing and I handed without the need to speak to him and took a seat, it must be fair to say that the guards depot barbers shop must have had the shiniest floor in any barracks in the world! I could not believe at the speed I was cut, trimmed, and ejected out of the chair "next! I remember looking in the mirror before I left and seeing my ears for the first time in a very long time and thinking it was funny.

When back outside I noticed a lad was having a talking to with Corporal HC, it turned out he did not want a haircut and was asking to go home, I thought Christ at this rate there will be no one left as both rooms were completely full, at least six extras beds were in the middle of both rooms so I think there must have been sixty of us and already three or four had gone home, and it was only the second day there. When everyone had finished hair cutting Corporal MG told us when we got back to the room we were going to start "Swabbing" yet more terms that made no sense to me anyway.

That afternoon we were shown where the cleaning cupboard and its contents were located and had a lesson in how to clean a toilet and toilet cubicle inclusive of how the toilet roll should be folded on the holder in each cubicle, the importance placed by Corporal MG that the "S" bend and any pipe work should be clean and free from dust and lastly that the brush and brush holder used to clean the inside of the bowl was to be free from shit. Corporal MG then moved onto how to clean the sinks inclusive of how many twists to the left around the cold tap that the chain holding the plug must be wound before hanging down within the bowl, if any one of the chains was slightly longer by being replaced the metal links should be removed to make sure it was the same length as all the rest, thereafter this had to be the same with all the plugs on all the sinks, a particular point to note from Corporal MG was the importance that was placed on ensuring that soap scum that can accumulate within the inside of the plastic plug must be cleaned and only plastic be visible.

We went onto the shower cubicles for more of the same the point to note here was to make sure that the soap holders were free from soap residue, and of course each room had a door the toilets, shower room and bathroom each having two brass hinges and these hinges had three brass screws holding them onto the doors, these had to be cleaned with metal polish and the centre of the brass wood screw free from dust and any metal polish residue.

There was what is known as a Blanco room, which was a room with a long and wide concrete top similar to a modern kitchen top that had a Belfast type sink and one cold tap at one end, this was for cleaning kit such as applying polish to boots etc, there was also a drying room which had three rows of benches with a rail running atop of them, similar to what you have in a sports changing room, this was to hang and dry wet clothing, wet boots, webbing etc.

There were several hot radiators located on the floor of the Blanco room guarded by a wire mesh similar in construction to a fire guard of old. The mirrors had to be cleaned as a matter of course and the screws holding the mirrors the same treatment. The floor had to be washed and cleaned and we were shown how to use the mop and bucket and to change the water regularly. I think you can get the picture, these tasks would be broken down and handed out on a rota system and you could be on Sinks one week, toilets or showers the next, for room inspection everyone did everything.

We were set about cleaning the ablutions as they were known all that afternoon, Corporal MG reminding us to put "Brasso " a metal polish on our list of things to buy after giving us a lid full of his own Brasso for the screws and hinges, he then went away and later pinned a "Swabbing rota" on the wall and from that, we, as I was not the only one confused at times by all the odd terminology being used now understood what Swabbing was.

I remember going to the sinks, others to the showers and to the bathroom etc, no one went into the toilet and Corporal MG actually had to tell some to get in there and sort them out, as I was cleaning my sink I could hear someone being sick in the bog as Corporal MG told them they must put their hand in the bowl and scrub under the rim I learned later that some excrement had sprayed from the bristles onto this lads face and he started retching and eventually threw up in the bowl, this as does often happen started a chain reaction and others started to throw up as well and Corporal MG became very angry and said he would chin, meaning punch the next fucker to throw up. I think some people swallowed their own vomit that day. It is worth remembering that at least 30 of us had been using these toilets for two days and this was the ablutions first real cleaning.

The next day we were woken much earlier than the day before by Corporal MG, I did not need waking up as I had been woken by some fool blowing a Bugle Somewhere in the camp repeatedly, this time the waking up was not by the light being put on above your head with a reasonable gentle shake of the foot! It was all the main lights being put on in the room and Corporal MG coming into the room and shouting that it was time to get up; this was odd as it was not like yesterday.

Corporal MG reminded us that Scoff was at 07:30 hrs I asked BG what time it was and he said it was 06:30 hrs, we all meandered into the ablutions in a slow procession walking as though we had no sleep at all, then the sound of "Song Sung Blue" by Neil Diamond started up and Corporal MG fully dressed ready to go came out of his bunk and started shouting that if we did not get a move on we would be late for breakfast and reminded us all that bed blocks needed making and the clock was ticking, I personally took this on board as I could see he was quite frustrated. Back at my bed I started to make my bedding block, it seemed so easy yesterday and I did not put as much effort in as I did yesterday when practicing but thought it would not matter as after all we were new.

After what seemed only five minutes Corporal MG told us to get outside as it was time to go to Scoff and again off, we doubled thank fully Corporal MG said I did not have to wear my tie which was a relief as some of the other recruits were wearing trousers and a shirt only my suit was getting well used I did not think Burtons ever thought it would be used as much! Scoff was the same as the days before and so were the rude swipes with aluminium ladles levied by the chefs onto your knuckles for trying to take two ladles of beans instead of one.

When we got back to the room all the beds were either on their sides or standing on headboards and the bed blocks were thrown all over the floor not recognisable as bedding blocks, as we returned to our bed spaces confused TM said to Corporal MG we had been burgled as all the clothing etc was gone from his locker, Corporal MG casually asking had he put a lock on it as he had told us all to do the day we arrived, he said he was not sure but it was an obvious burglary just look at the room ! Corporal HC could be heard shouting and raving across the corridor from our room at the recruits in the other room and then after hearing that door slam, he kicked ours open and started, "Right you fucking cretins need to wise up and speed up, if I ever find another locker unlocked again ill bounce you from here to the fucking sand hill" again I was wondering what bouncing and sand hill were? In any case he raved at all of us that we had let Corporal MG down and that all our bedding blocks were in "Shite order" and we better get them sorted and as we could not motivate ourselves in the morning, we would be getting up earlier from now on.!

After he went, we collectively started to reclaim what was hopefully our own bedding and re started making bedding blocks. Corporal MG was getting more and more angry that so far no one had started swabbing and we needed to speed up because if we did not, we would find life very difficult, he then took VR downstairs to Flanders II room and when he came back VR had to agree with him without the need for very much prompting that their room was immaculate and all toilets clean and beds made.

Corporal MG explained that we were going to be Issued with uniform today and that we need to make sure we knew what size head we were and waist etc; I did not have a clue as my mother had always bought my clothing. I distinctly remember that although it was September it was very warm even at that time of the morning as we all doubled to the QMs [Quartermasters] block. When we arrived, it was quite chaotic lots of shouting and shuffling recruits many still with long hair others like us newly crew cut.

We were told to form a queue those with surnames beginning A to D first est., which we did lining along the wall above a raised platform or loading bay. Corporal MG and Corporal HC then went inside and came out telling us that when called forward we should shuffle through the door and when asked to give our surname, initial, number, and platoon. I was ok with my name and platoon, but I had not even looked at my number since I had used it in the addressed to my parents at the insistence of Corporal MG.

After a few minutes the first five or six went through the door, but within minutes out came two of them flying through the same entry door chased by an angry looking Corporal HC, they did not have their numbers memorised and were being shouted at with fierce condemnation before being told to run back to the room and get their numbers, Corporal MG asked who else did not have their number memorised yet? No one after seeing the rollocking just given the last two unfortunates declared not knowing, I was almost at the front of the queue as my surname began with F, Corporal HC zeroing in on AE who although spluttering at times recited his number, then me and I thought I could make it up and started, 453217615 which was complete arse, Corporal HC took one pace forwards and dragged me out of the queue by the scruff of the neck my feet not touching the ground, and asked me if I was sure that was my number ? I decided the game must be up and said "no, I think that's it" and with that he pushed me towards the ramp leading down into the loading bay and told me to never ever try to be smart with him again and get my arse back to the to the block. Corporal MG asking the rest assembled did anyone else fancy bluffing it? And after a few seconds most of the platoon without prompting simply left the queue was running headlong towards the block to get the registration card from the room.

When we arrived back the first few Issued kit were walking back looking very odd and under pressure from the weight of kit and wearing what can only be described as "Flasher Macintosh coats" as seen in comic sketches by Benny Hill and wearing berets of the same likeness to boot, they were each carrying matching suitcases, and a green bag over the shoulder.

When it was my turn I took a step forward and was given a suitcase which was open the two keys put inside clearly for you to see, then you went to the left and two boots were put in after confirming your size next shirts jumpers and so on and so forth finishing with you trying on a number two dress and keeping that on followed by a beret and lastly the flasher Mac over that, a signature written and off you went as best possible doubling under the kit back to the room like a stream of ants occasionally giggling at each other.

When we got back to the room each of us started to put away the Issued kit into the cupboard, that was until Corporal MG eventually came back and told everyone to get the overalls we had been Issued on and the beret and get outside carrying your registration paper with you.

When we got outside we got what we now established normal form and "fell in" three ranks Corporal MG was joined by Corporal HC and the recruits from his room and each walked up to the first man and asked for the card, then the number to be repeated, if you got it correct you were told to get upstairs, if as the majority did get it wrong, you were told to put the number in your beret and get down in the press up position, and just for clarity Corporal MG showed what that was.

We, those who like me did not have the number memorised were ordered down into the press up position and told that on the upward push to recite the first of the eight numbers and on the down stroke look at the next number and on the up stroke call that number out, and off we went, down, up 2, down, up 4, down up 5 down, up 1, down, up 3, down up 6 down, up 4, down, up 4, and then again except we had to shout louder which was in audible as everyone had a different number, after 32 press up we were told to stand up and again both Corporal   s went along asking for the card and for the number to be recited, if correct upstairs, if wrong, "adopt the position "

After what seemed at least an hour of this only a few were left I am being one of them were told to stand up and close into a smaller squad. The rest of the platoon was called down stairs and told to start doing press with us until "we" meaning the small squad could recite our number; this caused a groan amongst the whole squad and off we all went up and down up and down, until stopped and asked to recite the number, now, I do not know much about body language but I do know angry faces when I see them and that was enough incentive for me to make sure I got it as I could see very bad repercussion's for this one, and thank god I know knew mine and was able to join the squad leaving only one or two who eventually after veiled threats from within the squad when doing press ups like me realised this could end badly for those causing the discomfort for the rest.

When I got back upstairs, I looked at myself in the mirror within the locker door and although it was just a pair of army green overalls and a unshaped ill-fitting beret, with my short hair army rank as a J/Guardsman and newly remembered army number I smiled as it dawned upon me I was actually becoming a soldier.

Moreover, a Guardsman.

Chapter IV

Daily, weekly routine in the depot.

If we thought the way we had packed our lockers away after the kit Issue was over, we were very much mistaken. That afternoon we were sent to find cardboard from every skip, or bin area we came across. It was odd as the NAAFI, cook house any place you looked had no empty boxes, neither had Sandies, the Sgts or Officers mess when we collectively returned, we only had a very small amount of scruffy water-stained parts of boxes. Corporal MG was cursing the "Gobblers" to Corporal HC, I had no idea what a "Gobbler" was but imagined it must have been the nickname for some sort of litter sweeping machine as the cursing was to do with the lack of cardboard.

Basically, the Grenadiers or "Gobblers" had obviously got around the camp looking for cardboard before us. In any case L/Sgt TC came to the rescue later in the afternoon when he came in and had several folded boxes he had picked up from home and around the married quarters where he lived basically an army housing estate.

A Gobbler is what I learned later to be the distasteful nickname for the Grenadier Guards, to be honest to this day I'm not sure why, moreover it was unofficially customary to spit on the ground when a Coldstreamers has to say the word Grenadier! It's worth saying here that they have a similar name for us "Sheep Shaggers" I think it has its origin due to some Coldstream guards raping some Nuns somewhere in the world in the 18th C.

We came took now the Household Calvary as "Donkey wallopers" and the Scots, Irish and Welsh guards as the colonials. The intake of Coldstreamers and Grenadiers was large enough to warrant two platoons solely of the same we are being Gib II and the Grenadiers, Gib I. The Scots, Irish and Welsh guards formed a composite platoon as the numbers were not as vast as ours for obvious size due to national population variance. We the Juniors I.e., up to age 17.5 years old were in the more modern part of the Guards Depot.

The older recruits again formed a collective of all 5 regiments and were in the older part of the camp and were called Caterham Company, when I used to see them, I wondered why such old men would join the Army, Old men being average age 21!

As juniors, we were kept as though at school we had leave along the same lines as six formers and we had training at the depot for 12 months whereas the older trainees in what was called Caterham Company were there for only six months the logic I think that they can absorb training faster than us juniors. I was always amused when I saw Caterham company on Drill as they did not have the luxury of 12 months slow but hard work on their boots and so they would be bees waxed (heated and hot wax poured on them) but not very well and the end of the boots from the toe cap always appeared bent upwards.

I arrogantly thought they were not as good as us due to only having six months in training the reverse was true as they had to cram all that into six months. There was also the Brigade squad these were potential Guards officers who did 8 weeks training in D lines under the same conditions as us prior to going to Sandhurst. They had it very hard, I had an exchange with a former then barrack room Corporal from the Scots Guards Corporal JJ in 1988 who at one stage had the Brigade squad carry all their metal lockers up to the top of the Sand Hill and its contents inclusive of beds and bedding and show them as though they were in the room.

After inspecting and finding faults throw most or all of it back down the Hill reminding them, they had a re show everything back where it had come from in an hours' time!

The mystery of the cardboard was soon over as Corporal MG set the room table into the centre of the room and went ahead to get TM to bring everything, he had been Issued over to him and alongside the table he set up the iron and ironing board. He explained and showed us how to initially assemble our 58-pattern webbing into what is called skeleton order i.e., not 100 % together as we would only need it like this for our basic skill at arms. We would gather and then return to our beds and do the same. TM all the time smiling as he was getting his tailor made for him as we went. This was going to take all day as it was a lengthy process and you had to get it right the hooks on the hangers had to face the same direction, the sleeves had to be two inches over the next item of clothing, the order for hanging the clothes had to be followed. All Brass on item would need to be cleaned sock trays dust free, and so it went on. The cardboard became a template to use inside PT vests and PT shorts; basically, the cardboard was cut to the width of the shelf, then marked equally marked in three placers with a ruler and folded to make three sides with an opening. This was placed inside the item of clothing and folded so that the front panel of the cardboard inside the PT vest Shorts etc was flat and free from crease and then slotted into the shelf, a colour code was used of Blue, Shorts, Red PT vest and Blue Shorts, with the white PT vest on another shelf as the guard's colours are Blue, Red, Blue. It was well into the evening that we were all still working way beyond lights out 22:00hrs so we went into the Blanco room, [utility room and put blankets on the window to hide the light and continued well into the small hours ironing and making lockers up.

A typical locker layout Guards Depot

In the morning Corporal MG woke everyone up and after washing and shaving came around and conducted his initial inspection with us all sleepy eyed and stood by our beds in overalls. He then went ahead to throw everything onto the floor locker by locker finding a fault or various faults as he went through. We could hear loud shouts from the Gobbler block and across the hall as the same was happening to everyone I suppose.

Then whoosh off to breakfast, on our return a further rollocking for leaving equipment un-secured and unlocked summarily sent out to run around the block with our tin helmets on, Suitcase in hand for x number of times and then back in.

It was no surprise I suppose that some were getting a bit fed up and I remember the delight on Corporal MGs face as a couple of lads went to his room and said they wanted to go home. They were told to pack up their kit and lock it away the problem was that the room was so full they had been sharing!

It was lessons then we were sent outside and were taken for drill. The first drill was marching around the camp in our new drill boots wearing overalls, the instructor calling out the time and stopping every now and then saying this is this place and that is that place and we went all over the camp. A fiver was promised to anyone who drove the heel into the ground hard enough to break the heel a challenge taken up by RA who using a pen knife whittled away at the heel of his boot later that night. It was no surprise then that he won that fiver twice until they caught on.

Life settled down and we soon got into the routine, up very early make bedding blocks only to have them thrown through the open window as they were never up to standard. The issue was that you had to strip down the bed sleep in it every evening and make the bloody thing before you went to breakfast, it left little time.

It was sometime later in the training I forget how long but, RA seemed to be ahead of the game all the time and always out through the door to scoff with perfect bedding block made, it transpired later he had gone through an open window in the Gobbler block during a break and stolen a bedding block, so he had one permanently made under his bed crafty git. Others took to sleeping on the floor in the army sleeping bag never to disturb the bedding block and get ahead in the morning.

We had inspection after inspection until we ran like clockwork, however, at times we would have little or no time between lessons, you could be in drill order in the morning and at 10:30 need to be in Skill at arms i.e. combats uniform skeleton webbing and have 30 minutes to change included in this we would have to have a mug of tea from the tea bucket, the tea bucket was literally a bucket and one person's job was to run with it to the cook house at break and fill it with tea, the same bucket we would clean with metal polish every night .

I remember Corporal MG was looking for me to take the tea bucket, knowing this would make me extremely late I hid inside my locker to the amusement of WD. After several times being late due to the compulsory tea break, we were told we still needed to speed up we were introduced to the delight of quick changing parades, these were an after normal days training activity usually carried out around 20:30 hours after shining parade, to optimise the fact that your locker and kit contained was immaculate and as it should be. Corporal MG would take of his watch and sit at the table and shout various times he thought it should take to get into what he called out and be stood to attention by your bed.

The parade would cease when everyone was stood as ordered in the time, "3 *Minutes, three minutes, Boots drill, Long Johns, String Vest, Poncho Steel helmet holding small mess tin left hand large in the right Gooooo ! "* so off we would go like possessed by demons tearing into our lockers dragging out neatly folded clothing starched and pressed ed, only to hear *" 15 seconds, 10 seconds, 5, 4, 3 2 1, Stop to slow, 5 minutes 5 minutes Pumps electric PT, barrack dress trousers, 2 dress   shirt and tie, Raincoat, Foraged cap, skeleton webbing Goooo!"and so on and so forth.*

Thankfully and after everything was wrecked, he'd say ok get some sleep room and locker inspection after scoff i.e., breakfast. You were lucky to get it all back in by silly o`clock circa 03:00 hrs and then right on time but a little earlier this time at 05:30hrs we were ordered outside to do regimental blanket shaking.

This is where you take all your blankets outside and in three ranks shake the blankets to get them dust, and species free, this is done to drill time called out and the end results is much coughing and wheezing, this would be done periodically as a punishment along with changing parades, but it did work we got faster we learned to get motivated and "cut about" all the time and nearly every day someone would just say Fuck this after their bed block went through the window or half way through a quick changing parade and quit, much to the delight of Corporal MG and Corporal HC who were in some sort of contest.

Shining parades

The shining parades were held in the evenings, after dinner, we dressed in overalls with a poncho stretched over the bed and the suitcase forming a working shelf at the bottom of the bed underneath the same. We laid out our boot's bayonets forage caps and buff belts and polished cleaned for at least an hour, during these parades we sat legs across the bed.

During shining parades, we had what was called regimental history instruction, moreover, learn and remember depot & regimental Battalion staff. Corporal MG would read out some pages and then we would be evaluated or questioned starting at one bedspace to the next so you would be asked with no idea what questions might be a typical Question would be,

> *"Fish how many Victoria Crosses does the Regiment have?*
> "Answer 13, phew,
> *"BG what's the name of the Depot Commandant?"*
> Answer "I don't know Cpl".
> *"But I just told you "*
> "I can't remember Cpl".
> "Ok come here".

What would happen now would never happen these days you were punished by Bumper, a Bumper is a heavy weight attached to a pole for polishing floors see photo, this pole was very heavy, it had to be to hold such a weight and undertake such work, it was obviously used in a pendulum motion and the offender would Kneel head bowed, and the pole was then kicked across the pendulum impacting on the person's head. He could then return to his bed.

> *"BG, what's the name of the depot Commandant?"*

Answer

"Lt Col D.R.P. Lewis WG."

This is proof that bumper reminders do work! It was very surprising that RA was becoming an expert in regimental history hardly ever getting anything wrong, he let me in on his secret he had written most of the regimental and depot personalities onto a piece of paper and had folded it concertina style and taped it underneath his bed side light on shining parade he would lean back out of sight and pull it down read out the answer, sit upright again, the paper shortened itself and going back out of sight due to the concertina effect to the underside of the lamp.

An Older picture taken in D-lines possibly Caterham company of a shining parade.

J/LCpls WD & VR left.

Another term for my new-found vocabulary was purging it seemed to the staff that we were always purging [moaning] and a suitable punishment was found, these punishments were introduced over the first 8 weeks we were there I wondered what more they could come up with? I did not have long to wait; the Sand hill run was a blinder. At the western end of the camp was the old camp near Elizabeth barracks called D Lines the sort of camp you see in old WWII films it was found as you headed out towards the ranges there just before the training area was a very, very steep hill called the Sand hill.

It was not un-common that a changing parade could go bad as the time taken was not achieved and the assembled mass considered idle even though we were always tired.

Tiredness leads to moaning and under the breath mutterings or purging, about 4 weeks in and with our boots getting to quite a good standard our

buff belts and brass taking shape we had a changing parade and the order of dress called out along with "5 minutes. 2 dress, drill order!" this was quite upsetting as we had just polished everything suddenly in just under an hour of the usual madness getting into one set of kit to another when back in 2 dress, we were all shouted at to get outside. We were then running in three ranks towards what is called the Sandhill.

As Corporal HCs squad was behind us doing the same told me this must be have been pre-planned, anyway off we went running in full two dress towards the direction of the ranges, this was well past 20:00 hrs 8pm and as the sight came into view of the Sand hill surely not I thought as we headed towards it, but as so often what seemed like madness to me was perfectly normal for the Guards Depot.

We halted and we were with all the usual shouting told "get up that fucking hill last man up and down will be heading home Gooooo!" and off we went with a warning not to get our kit dirty! The punishment lasted over an hour and at the end a question was asked did anyone have any more purging to do about the quick changing parades? None was forthcoming, and back we marched and again everything had to be cleaned ready for the morning.

The Sandhill many a trainee Guardsman has sweated at all hours on this beggar in many varied orders of dress!

We soon became used to running up and down that hill at one time after midnight in nothing more that string pants, string vest, Army plimsolls and wearing to top it all off a tin hat wearing gas masks.

It was not all gloom as we were young, we could have a hobby night and I chose war gaming found in the Army education block. It was only

75

an hour, but it was good to get out of the room as the constant cleaning of rooms and equipment was relentless. We also had the NAAFI shop, and a local religious shop called Sandies Soldiers home where you could seek solace from one of the volunteer ladies that ran tea and cakes, who also charged well over the odds for cleaning kit there was also the WRVS women, [Women's Royal Voluntary Service] Grannies mostly located in a room near the NAAFI, you could see at times some trainees having a good cry on their shoulder!

We also had the odd cinema night again a Commandant's directive and at least once every two weeks we could all march as a depot to the SKC cinema located in D Lines camp and see a film, I remember seeing "The odd angry shot" and "The wild Geese" in addition we were treated one night to a west end show the whole depot went, I believe at the commandants own expense to see Chicago, never to be invited again as apparently all the mini viewing binoculars were stolen. I very fondly remember one of the Guards bands came and played all the regimental marches each one preceded by being called out by the RSM to the roar of the whole depot cheering their regimental March both slow and quick time this is what the fast-marching speed and the slow one you see at funerals etc. is called.

We were taught the 24-hour clock on shinning parades having to come forward look at the hands of the room clock adjusted by the barrack room instructor and call out its AM or PM equivalent in 24-hour time, it was a great thing for me as on my first leave home I now understood the train and bus timetables! However, in the main we even worked on Sundays however we did get a lie in.

The morning routine each day was the same up at 05:00hrs possible regimental blanket shake, shower, shave, rush to get bedding blocks done get your swabbing job done, march to scoff walk back, repair the room if it had been assaulted or collect bedding blocks from downstairs, remake re learn get ready for the first lesson and be in the correct equipment. Then outside for area cleaning picking up litter around the accommodation and our area of responsibility and sweeping up the roadsides.

Me far left beret and cigarette in hand.

I am not sure how far into training this was taken but it must be a few months as Junior rank has been given to J/LCpl WD

Chapter V

Drill, drill, drill & fifth week inspection.

"The aim of drill is to produce a Guardsman who is alert and obedient, to provide the basis of good teamwork. The purpose of formal parade ground drill is to enable bodies of Guardsmen to be moved easily and quickly from point to point in a smart and soldierly like manner."

That is what the manual says, or words to that effect, but to us drill was bloody hard work filled with accompanying bouts of terrific punishments.

After we had spent the first week, what was commonly called Z week, we started drill without weapons, basically foot drill. We had to get to a certain standard for our 5-week inspection. If we made the grade, we would have our first long weekend on leave.

The drill started really from the first night as I said learning to stand up and to attention when an NCO [Sergeant / Corporal] or officer walked in the room.

We did drill everywhere, in the queue for the barbers, marching to scoff initially in our coveralls, we were always doing drill, you never walked in the depot you marched, even on your own going to the NAAFI you marched. It was a constant round of springing to attention and saluting doing eyes left or right, asking permission for self and others to fall in or out turning left or right and bending the knee and bashing it down.

The first sessions of drill are done to what the Army calls regimental time, in essence when you moved after the pre curser instruction you shouted 1, stood still and shout 23, then move and finalise on shouting 1 again e.g., 1 pause 23 pause 1 and as the foot strikes the ground just shouted PUNCH!

The words the instructors would use were colourful and at times humorous to say the least. When entering the drill square the drill instructor always halted us a saluted at times no one was present I learnt later it was simply protocol. If we were looking down whilst marching you get funnies like "stop shagging looking down there's no money, the Jocks, e.g., Scots Guards were here earlier and picked the ground clean". Also, encouragement, "stop looking down lift your heads up swing your arms parallel to the ground or I will rip your arm off pull out an eye and skull fuck you to death with the soggy end of your arm, be warned" LOOK up!

We were never allowed on the main drill square in those first few weeks as we were too junior, we ended up on the small square or car park by drummer's practise classrooms not far from our block, it was next door to the gym. The rationale was that way we could be kept from the ever-critical eyes of drill sergeants and the Regimental sergeant major who had offices in the Kremlin found at the top of the main square.

In many ways things have changed in training in the British army however one thing has always remained a constant and that's drill. This is because the army has perfected how to teach drill through a teaching script, I learnt years later my NCOs course, it covers any manner of drill movements and after a while its imprinted on your brain even as a recruit being taught you soon learnt it, always starting with.

"Taking you a stage further in your Foot/ Rifle drill,
I will now teach you the Left turn at the halt [or it might be] about turn on the march,"

The basic way they taught you was EDIP, Explanation, Demonstration, Imitation, Practice. We did not march at a nice steady pace, we marched around like madmen on speed, we marched at a speed of 180 paces a minute. The Platoon sergeant carried a pace stick with him on drill which is like a metronome for music in so much as it was a precise instrument of a pace between feet distance when marching.

It was essentially two joined sticks that open on a hinge at the top with a brass slide running between them making an A shape.

The brass between could be set to 180 paces a minute through to slow march of 30 paces per minute. The Sergeant would march switching the point on the ground between the tips whilst his feet kept in time with the twisting pace stick, it's quite a skill, the pace stick also made a very good spear when thrown from a distance at you if you messed up.

We had so many variations of dress i.e., clothing it was hard to keep track, for drill in the winter we wore our second-best boots as we had two pairs one was best and the other were normally equally as good, but you did the drill practice in them more than the best. The hobnail boots had leather laces which were to run flat untwisted through the loopholes and highly polished. We wore dark green trousers called barrack dress, with a khaki lightweight cotton shirt tie and what was called a heavy-duty jumper over the shirt with a green plastic belt with plastic bayonet frog over the jumper complete with forage cap. If it was raining, we had mackintosh raincoats like Humphrey Bogart in one of his 40s films.

In the summer for drill, we wore the same but with an open neck green itchy shirt called a KF shirt sleeves rolled up the width of a fag packed to four fingers. I hated them as they were so rough, they rubbed you under the arms and the back. As time went on as the buff belts became whiter and presentable so we wore them for drill instead of the plastic belt I think it was a bit "chippy regiment" to wear the plastic belt. In any case it looked smart. Our best dress was number two dress this looks similar to what the soldiers wore in WW1 and WW2 khaki trousers jacket shirt tie and braces, never ever, ever, forget the braces.

What we learned in those few weeks was what was required to pass the 5th week inspection. The first part was the fitting and cleanliness of the equipment with massive attention to detail by the inspecting officer. This was normally the Depot Adjutant followed by the entourage of the Regimental Sergeant major and Drill sergeants who did the real checking you out!

I knew you had to fear these people but at times they could be human and walk over before an inspection and wish you luck or even give some re assurance. As it was often, we were terrified. Why? If you failed this inspection, you would be back squadded, which means you would not pass. Moreover, when the platoon came back from the incumbent leave you would start all over again with the new recruits who had just come of the train and repeat the whole 5 weeks again with them.

The test was on the main drill square dressed in our smartest number two dress. The test started with us being in an unorganised rabble chatting on one side of the drill square in a kind of casual mass. The first thing was a Sergeant from our platoon would walk to the middle of the square and shout Fall In! to which we stopped what we were doing and marched over to the front of him as individuals loosely formed three ranks, obviously we had pre practised where we were to go before hand. However, the next word of command was tallest on the right, shortest on the left, we responded by organising ourselves into a straight line with the tallest man on the left as you looked at us or the right looking ahead of us.

The Sergeant would march and stand in front as a judge of heights and move one person to the left or to the right until we were in a sloping line tallest on the right shortest on the left as he looked at us. Then he would shout from the right number! we would call out one after the other the tallest person being #1 on his left #2 on his left #3 and so on and so forth down the line until the last man would shout his number followed by "last man Sir!" if an officer was on parade.

The sergeant would shout odd numbers one pace forwards even numbers one pace rewards March! the result being you ended up in two lines, he would then shout, "number one stand, the remainder, front rank to the right re rank to the left, left and right turn". The result we were looking at the back of the head of the person in front of you.

The sergeant marched over to the tallest, e.g., the #1 or from now on called the right marker shout "quick March" we would all set off together marching behind each other like a snake heading towards the right-hand man or #1 the Sergeant would say front centre rear rank to you as you passed him indicating what rank you should be in.

The result was we were back in three ranks front centre and rear as before the platoon ended up with the taller on the edges and the shorter in the centre concave as you look at us.

The Sergeant would walk back in front and centre facing you about 25 paces. The sergeant would then shout, "Right Marker!" very loud and with a certain amount of violence or anger in his voice. In unison we would all brace up meaning stood tall chest out ready to stand to attention when the order came. The command was in its fullness for the right-hand man only, he would spring to attention and set off on his own marching 14 paces straight ahead of us, he would then halt on the 14th pace then stand at ease as we were 14 paces behind him.

The sergeant would then shout, "get on parade", to which we all sprung to attention together including the right hand man after short pause we all marched forward marching together stepping out with the left foot first counting in our heads with each step 1,2,3,4,5,6,7,8, 9,10,11,12,13 ending on 1, 2 being number 14 at the halt all together, it sounds simple but you all have to be together.

He would then shout in open order right dress; the front rank would take a short sharp pace forward with the left foot back to attention and the rear rank the same going backwards. The centre rank did not move their feet only their heads like the whole platoon after a pause to the right.

He would then march to the right of the right marker or #1 and start telling you as an individual by name to move forward a little or backwards until he was happy with the straightens of the line or file, he would shout stand still the front rank, he would then turn left march the correct distance for open order between ranks or files and do the same for the centre rank and the rear rank.

All the time the adjutant and entourage would be writing comments on clip boards......well that's what was supposed to happen, and how we practiced it for weeks.

In our case when we had all marched from the rabble and were ready to march on the command "Get on Parade", A N Other sprung to attention with such force or enthusiasm that his trousers fell to the ground settling around his boots, the remainder of us marched ahead regardless and with the same enthusiasm to Impress on the 14th step I halted but immediately my left heel struck the ground I slipped ending up on my back completely prone.

The platoon was left trying to stifle the giggles as the Regimental sergeant major came over first, not with a how are you? Let me help you up but shouting at me on the floor dazed "that is not the way you show the adjutant you have 13 studs in each boot sole, get up, get up and the whole entourage started screaming at us except the adjutant who had turned his back shoulders moving up and down obviously also laughing.

We were ran of the drill square to the edge to regain composure, A N Other was asked if he had his braces on he replied yes but after a quick

85

feel through the number two dress jacket it turned out he was lying….he was sprinted off to gaol faster that a ferret down a rabbit hole. As for me I was asked what I was doing? one sergeant asking another mockingly to get on the phone and ask if the Olympic committee knew that one half of Torvel and Dean was in the army learning a new routine called "fuck up my parade" I was crest fallen and knew that I was going to be back squadded.

However, one of the Depot Drill sergeants came over I think he was Welsh Guards, called me over with the Platoon sergeant. I marched over and stood to attention awaiting the rollocking, but none came, he said to me I was in an elite club as he had done the same thing on Tower Guard a few years ago in front of hundreds of tourists. He told me to forget it, get myself together for the retest. He told the platoon Sergeant no recriminations to be made against me and to be back on the square to try again in 5 minutes. The platoon Sergeant said you are very lucky, I thought you were on the train home!

In any case we tried again and proved to the adjutant we knew the basic foot drill without weapons. It goes without saying we worked up to that test over those weeks along with the other training such as Map reading, endless kit cleaning, fitness, Skill at arms i.e., weapons training and field craft, more of which later in the book.

The test was relatively simple, after we had "got on parade" we were inspected and notes taken on good or bad turnout, every other man was asked either to "Show me your note book and pen" to which you took a short step back with you left foot, stamping in down at an angle behind the right foot heel, undone your right breast pocket and showed it the pencil had to be sharpened at both ends. It might be you were asked for your ID card or to lift your right or left boot off the ground when the officers was behind you so that he could check you had polished the instep and sole of your boots, and that you had the full thirteen studs in the sole.

In addition, you would be asked a regimental history question, all RA had to do was lean back and look under the bedside lamp for the answer but luckily, and we all had the scars on our foreheads from the swinging arm of the bumper on shining parades to prove it, coupled with endless nights cleaning the kit whist answering and learning the regimental history we were up to standard on the inspection.

After the last man was inspected permission to carry on was requested of the Adjutant and given, the parting words from the Adjutant were heard, which was him saying to the Platoon Sergeant all good well done.

It was now for the drill inspection it was so practiced we all knew it off by heart as you can see, I can recall it from almost 45 years ago. Fundamentally we had to obey commands such as "turning at the halt, left turn, Right turn, about turn," marching in front of the adjutant towards the left end-ding with a saluting command, "salute to the front Salute!" Which involved us all halting and saluting all together in time. Then an about turn without prompting and stepping off again marching in the other direction to the right of the adjutant only this time "saluting, salute to the right Salute!" followed by another about turn and this time marching in the other direction and "saluting, salute to the left Salute!" whilst still marching. We also showed we could change step a drill movement to get you back in step if you lost it within the squad, it's a kind of skip!

We then broke into slow time which slowed things down, slow time is the slow march that you see on funerals etc we did the same thing only no saluting just about turning and doing a change step as we had done in quick marching. Lastly, we would get the order break into quick time, count four paces Quick March! and resume at the same pace as before.

When we were in front and centre of the Sergeant taking the drill session he would halt us, turn us to our left facing him, he then in turn would turn about to face the Adjutant and march forward a few paces from him salute and say words to the effect, "that concludes the basic foot drill test for Gibraltar two Sir, do you wish to see more?" The reply being "no thank you", He would then ask permission to march the platoon of the square? The answer was always polite "Please do". We felt elated, well I certainly did on the march back to the barrack room all that hard work had paid off we had earned our short upcoming leave.

I was called intro the platoon office by a grenadier Sgt I forget his name he had me sit down and ask why I was there I tried to explain about always wanting to be a soldier my family having all been in the military etc, he cut me short and asked why then was I always holding back? I looked puzzled he went on to tell me that this discussion was for him independently to decide whether I should be back squadded.

My heart turned to stone. I asked what I had done wrong and he explained that on PT and many other examples where they knew I had not given 100% I explained that I was always worried about becoming totally exhausted and wanted to keep something back for example on the log run they and I knew it was correct that I was only very intermittently carrying it on my shoulder letting the others on the log take most of the strain I knowing full well if I repositioned myself Id have carried more of the weight. I asked for another chance and promised and assured him I would always try 100% from then on Sgt

McM nicknamed me I try hard, after that as I did give everything, to be honest I got fitter the harder I tried.

When I got back to the room, I kept it quite what it had all been about in the office, we had to clean all the kit again before getting away. You had to leave anything with brass on it covered in a light coating of Brasso or Duroglitt, you left your boots covered in a layer of un-shined polish. The bedding block had to be put in the lockers with pillows the room cleaned and after inspection by the beds you stood in civilian clothing, I was absolutely shocked how much weight I had lost It must have 2 stone or 28Lbs my suit was so ill fitting I used the army issued braces as my suit had the buttons for it so that I could keep the trousers up, the only other difference from how I arrived was that my civilian shoes now shined like a new penny !

I was not foolish enough to pack my number two dress to take home in my bag, I hid it all in an empty locker downstairs and I was right to do so as the first thing they the instructors did was open all our bags and dragged the uniform out!

I retrieved my uniform after we were told to go from the downstairs locker, I had a photo taken in it standing by my grandfather's fireplace in Gorleston on sea, but it was lost years ago, or I would have put it in this book.

Above 5th week inspection. I am third in from the right.

I have though included a photo booth picture of me and BG on that leave taken at Liverpool St station.

First Leave.

Me and BG who was is an Essex boy going on leave.

I remember the feeling of energy I had when travelling through the London underground from Waterloo to Liverpool Street station instead of the escalators I would run with suitcase in hand up them I was so fit. I exchanged my warrant to travel and boarded the train full of Men in suits and thinking how they can wear such smart suits, but the shoes be in such an unpolished state!

I would also look at people's hair sometimes greasy and think dirty flesh. Moreover, and even worse I told the man at the buffet car handling sandwiches he needed to clean his fingernails as he was a health hazard to me and all the people who might buy food of him.

I was so happy when the announcer would call out the next stops and I would understand the 24-hr time. I used the bus home and even though it felt like 5 minutes since I had been away Great Yarmouth market looked so desolate. But I went over to get some mushy peas anyway, but the stall was closed, I had and still do always make a bee line for the mushy peas stall in Great Yarmouth market.

I had what was known as credits in my pocket I.e., cash that was left over after the food accommodation and the weekly £5.00 were taken from my pay, I think we were on about £ 170.00 PM before stoppages an independent source I looked up stated that, in 1979 - average male non-manual wage age 21 and over - £113 per week (£5,876 pa). Anyway, I had some money in my pocket not as much as I would have liked but who ever does, I do remember 20 cigarettes was 25p.

After I got home I for an unknown reason felt odd, out of place. I have no idea to this day why, before I joined us teenagers in the village used to sit in the Bus stop talking mostly as there was not much to do when the youth club was not open. When I got off the bus sure enough it was the same. I said hello to all of them and we agreed to go to the pub, together we all walked to the Norsemen pub only for me to be welcomed home by the landlord but all of us told to leave as we were, and well we knew it were underage!

My mother had made my bed and I sat at the dining table my brothers and alike asking questions which I gave answers to most of the time except had I killed anyone yet! In the morning, I was awake at 05:00hrs unable to sleep so I'd make my bed with hospital corners, hoover, and dust the room take a bath, clean the bath and sink, mop the floor etc! My family did not appreciate the early morning routine at all, but I think my mother was glad of the extra swabbing. I went out with my old school friend up to Hemsby beach sea dell club met a local girl from Martham village who I believe would never have had anything to do with me before I joined up, but I had a newfound confidence and opinion of myself.

The romance lasted for a single fumbling outside and freezing near the Hotel Hermanus unbeknown to me she was in a relationship with a lad from Martham who I had been in school with, and so started my run of bad relationships with the opposite sex! The odd thing was after a few days I wanted to get back to the depot how crazy was that? I was only home for a few days and enjoyed the peace and quiet just before I went back, I found the inevitable red reminders for the gas and electricity bills went to town and paid them with Cash, I also sent a postal order via the post office to one on mums catalogues not telling my parents until after I had got back to the depot.

When I returned from leave we continued as before with training the only difference was the increase in tempo but without having to shout 1, 23, 1 out loud except for learning drill with weapons such as the Self Loading Rifle (SLR) and the Sub Machine gun or (SMG) to this day I cannot understand why I found rifle drill so hard to get, and the quality of our Platoon Sgt as an instructors comes through, Sgt R McM could see I was struggling with coordination but failing badly, he called me over to one side of D Lines square which was a drill square at the other end of the depot and was used by us sometimes for drill. He asked me without shouting what was wrong and he realised I was petrified as I could not get it straight away, and all I could think about was being gaoled for getting it wrong he could see I was trembling. He put his pace stick down and went through the shoulder arms through to the present and back with me for about 5 minutes and I got it as he constantly said not to worry if I got wrong and eventually of course I was able to do the drill movement well, he said I tried hard and should be called I try Hard. He did leave me with a warning though, in as much as now I had conducted the rifle drill movement in front of him correctly woe betide me if I now got it wrong in the squad.

Throughout the rest of the year drill increased to left and right forming and open and close order whilst in slow time in three ranks whilst marching for the passing out parade, drill in pairs and as an individual simulating being on sentry as conducted at all the Royal palaces. We practiced reversing arms for funerals, forming 2 ranks for street lining on the side of the Mall for and on the trooping of the colour, lastly grounding and taking up arms, fixing, unfixing bayonets.

It is fair to say by the time of our passing out parade irrespective of passing the depot Commandants inspection for rifle drill in an equivalent way to foot drill like our previous drill inspection by the Adjutant we knew in ourselves we were ready for Battalion and Queens Guards.

It was an extremely hard year in terms of drill practice, but it was explained to us what made us different to the rest. It was after our return from Thetford Battle camp that several members of the platoon tried out for, and some joined the Corps of Drums, they still did all the military training as us but, in the evenings, did Flute, Side drum and Bugle practice.

The Guards have always had a very good reputation for fighting skills in all the wars, indeed many might say we were the 18th C special forces I'll leave that open for debate, but the fact remains as was once said by a Navy Man through and through Lord Mountbatten, about being accepted by the lifeguards as an honorary Colonel was the most agreeable surprise he had ever had. He praised their military reputation from Waterloo to spearheading the British army from Normandy to Germany.

I cannot find the source but there was a saying akin to, "Sleep tight lads, the Guards are on the line." In reference to WW1 Trenches. It is open to debate, but military historians might argue that discipline, attention to detail from the drill square attributes much to success in battle.

Chapter VII

Skill at arms

It is not only being able to march in a straight line that makes a Guardsmen! professionalism, courage and skill with infantry weapons are crucial, the same EDIP teaching mantra used to teach us weapons discipline and safety when using them.

Skill at arms was always in Skellington order for training here we are outside the block in Skellington order picture taken from my window. I am third from the left rear rank.

Skill at arms [SAA]started straight away after our first leave. We would always wear Skellington order webbing in the class room when training with weapons but have to have full [CEFO] Central European fighting order webbing on for field craft so it might be we have 30 minutes between lesson's an example being SAA, SLR, [FN Self-loading rifle] lesson one followed Field craft Lesson one duties of a sentry in the field challenging pass words, so between that you had to put all the remaining pouches gas mask water bottle etc on the webbing for Fieldcraft and this is one reason our lockers were always in need of straightening up we were constantly changing.

I remember that SAA always taught in a classroom within D lines, I also remember how excited I was to start this training. So much so that on lesson one the classroom was set out with a straight line of chairs with an SLR placed underneath the chair, we went in and the first thing I did was get the rifle from under the chair resulting in a roar of verbal abuse by L/Sgt TB the instructor moreover being violently manhandled out the classroom door.

The accompanying punishment also included the whole class for my mistake was having to run around and around the training spiders which were the type of incredibly old 1940 style Nissan huts accommodation in D lines. They look a bit like H blocks of Northern Ireland infamy. I forget how many times, but it would have been until we were coughing and wheezing. The reason for the punishment was that we or I had no idea what safety state the rifles were in.

After calming down we were told that all the weapons in the room had been checked as safe prior to the lesson by the instructor the first lesson was naming all the parts of the rifle from the butt to the flash eliminator several times until we had it mostly remembered by the instructor holding the rifle and pointing at each part with a pencil. We were then allowed to put the weapons on our laps and in pairs point out question and answer each other over what this? pointing at a part of the weapon and what was the purpose, nothing else could be taught until we all spoke the same language if you like. We learnt how to check each weapon was safe and then how to strip them down in the correct way and even did it blind folded whilst being timed also filling magazines both in light and dark most of the time from the inside of your beret so they would not go all over the place.

It was the same with all weapons we would use as Guardsmen, Pistols, General purpose machine gun, Grenades right through to the 84MM anti-tank weapon and all types of ammunition. The culmination of this was to classify or pass your weapons tests before ever even shooting.

84 MM Carl Gustave anti-tank

GMPG Machine gun 7.62 mm

FN Self-loading rifle SLR 7.62mm

SMG Sub machine gun 9mm

Browning 9mm pistol   **L2 hand Grenade**

We learnt to shoot on an indoor range with Heckler Koch conversion kits put inside body of the SLR taking the calibre down to 22 rimfire. This was an innovative idea but gave you a misguided understanding of the power of the 7.62mm that the SLR was supposed to fire. The resulting shock for myself was measurable by the bruising on my shoulder after I first fired 7.62mm through them on Bisley range.

We had an excellent team of four soldiers come from the Army School of infantry to teach us about the penetrative power of all our weapons accompanied by an SKC made short films of the GPMG taking down a small wall and demolition of a car. The idea was to get out of our heads all the nonsense from Hollywood films. I still use and understand the principles of powder type and ratio combined with differing bullet heads in weight on the Parabellum of a 7.62 mm N or 308 as it is more commonly known as I still shoot a privately owned SLR at a civilian rifle club.

The SAA test were all pretty much the same for all weapons in principle, you would walk in to a room and the examiner would be at a table and tell you to bring him the weapon you were being tested on the Rifle, Pistol, SMG, GPMG Machine Gun, 66mmm rocket launcher, and the Carl Gustav 84 MM Anti-tank weapon or Charlie G as we called it would be in the middle of the class room floor or propped against a wall.

The first thing was not to pick it up but feel the location of the safety catch and check it was on. Then take control of the weapon by adopting the prone position e.g., on your belly on the floor behind the weapon and have point of the weapon in a safe direction. Then remove any ammunition i.e., the magazine. You would cock and check the chamber where the bullet would be pick up a round if there was one ejected and release any mechanism take of the safety catch, then fire of the energy or firing pin, re apply the safety catch and walk up to the inspecting NCO check the safety so he could see, cock open the weapon and angle the opening of the chamber so he could see it was clear and after he affirmed it was safe you release the energy or firing mechanism forward into the breach pull the trigger after pointing in a safe direction, re apply the safety catch. You would then be run through a series of things that can go wrong and the remedies for them.

We were shown a film I still remember it called, "An unthinking moment" it was black and white, but it showed a group of soldiers in a barrack room after shooting on the range cleaning their weapons and one pointing his weapon at another mockingly thinking it was clear and shot his mate! It was sobering stuff. I distinctly remember when we were doing our first pistol shoots at a hundred meters standing position and the big grin, I had on my face here I was 16 years old with a real live firing 9mm pistol. RA shouted eat your heart out Body and Doyle between shots until he was told to stop it.

It was no surprise to me really that on my third or penultimate leave from the depot I felt I had absolutely nothing in common with my old school friends at the bus stop and never would again with the average civilian, imagine being 16 and shooting an anti-tank missile at an old WWII tank on a range, let alone the cost!

The ranges at the depot were fantastic, we had an ETR range, Electric target range, meaning when you hit the target at various ranges the thing fell and then popped back up and gave you a score on what was called your APWT Annual personal weapons test. I have to say it even though it sounds Ostentatious, but I really was a particularly good shot and always got awarded the marksman badge.

I have no idea why NBC training was part of Skill at arms, but it was a lengthy part of our training. In classrooms we learnt the diverse types of chemical agents their use and how they were delivered to the battlefield. We watched films showing how Agent Orange used in Vietnam was supposed to kill the vegetation only but was also killing the wildlife and local population years later.

We also watched films about how the blisters would form on hands and arms of the volunteers who went to Porton Down chemical war fare labs in Salisbury Wiltshire. It was a very frightening subject. However, we were also trained in how to protect ourselves with special made trousers and jackets that covered you top to toe with added gloves, boots, and Gas mask. The trick was to "Mask in 9" meaning 9 seconds, I have no idea why 9 seconds as fast as you bloody could get the gas mask on first the suit next. I did not have much confidence as we were shown what would happen to you if just a pin heads worth of nerve agent got on your skin, just a pin head, this stuff would rain down like a shower when delivered by artillery, anyway it was all we had and the NAP tablets we were to take to help counteract the chemicals prior to war and Eppie pens, more like Olympic javelins which you were supposed to stab into your thigh and inject antidote to the gas agent.

And of course, as many a solider will remember the Gas chambers in training, I've spoken to several ex-soldiers from different regiments about this training and it depends on who you ask, but some had lessons where you never got a whiff of gas and others like us who were left choking for hours after the lesson was used for fun and games by the instructors.

The Gas chamber at the Guards Depot located at the top right of the Main drill square by the Drummers instruction block. This door must hold the record for the most punched, kicked door in the world.

The practical aspect of the training was to go to the Gas Chamber already in NBC Suits or Noddy suit. You had everything on including full CEFO tin helmet the only thing you did not have was your Gas mask.

After a briefing about the Gas used in this training would not kill you it would only make you "slightly" uncomfortable around the eyes if you got gas in them. We went in groups of 6-8 and the shout would go out Gas, Gas, Gas! To which we all put on Gas masks and with the breath you had taken before hand blew out hard after putting the mask on to expel any gas that had got in when masking up. It was then a buddy, buddy check to make sure the hood was fitted around the mask. The door was then open in you went all walking around and around one behind the other in a circle. It was after a few minutes more Gas tablets were lit in the middle of the room, and it got very foggy very quickly, but I was ok.

A lot of things never made any sense to me at times in the Army, I could smell a little gas and some inside my mask was getting in I was a little agitated and the instructor said it was normal to get a little gas in the mask!

NOW you tell me, if that's the case and it only takes a pin head of nerve agent on your skin to kill you why were these masks allowing a little gas in? Anyway, after the room was full of gas the instructors told us to take out our water bottles and he was going to demonstrate the technique for drinking water we had of course already done this in the classroom. You took out fuller's earth paper impregnated with a talc and powder around the bottle top then open the top take a deep breath lift the mask and take a mouthful of water and very quicky replace the mask. In my group everyone seemed to survive this, much I think, to the disappointment of the staff. The next test was to eat a small amount of biscuit, same process again, same result all managed to survive.

Then we had to take a deep breath and individually when pointed at lift the mask and shout our Army serial number, rank, name, regiment, and date of birth. This did the trick and the second or third person went berserk as the gas went into his lungs as he took a breath. It really was very, very disconcerting watching him fight with two instructors to get to that door, screaming it was terrifying. ok my turn, I sucked in air until my lungs could burst, and as quick as you like had the whole requirement spurted out closing the mask around my face blew for all I was worth to get the Gas out. The next person not so lucky and more screaming and scrabbling for the door eventually let out. We then played musical canisters; the canister is the filter on the side of the Gas mask it unscrews so that you can refresh the old one after so many days. After we had unscrewed our canister putting our hand over the opening left, we put them on the floor the instructors made us walk around again one behind the other but had removed one canister and when they shouted go you had to get a canister and screw it back on, of course one canister would be missing, that poor bastard again running at the door eventually it being opened, this went on and I eventually ended up the same.

The floor outside of the door was slippery with sick, in the small copse of trees nearby was junior Guardsman trying to recover their composure. The birds at every chance would gather and fly down for the free meal. I had passed but those who had tried to run out etc were told to join the next group. It was a gruesome scene, I thank the almighty that no one ever used real gas against me, but one thing I can say if I needed a shit in that environment my trousers would have simply stayed up. I'd have carried that mess around me in my pants until I had chance to change than risk it, I had no confidence in it. The same with thirst and eating no way would I ever take that chance until I was in a safe place to do so.

106

Chapter VIII

Fitness training

In the first few weeks at the depot our fitness well certainly my own extra few pounds were arguably stripped off by the constant marching at 3 million miles an hour on the drill square on and off it.

We did Physical training in one form or another every day, some was designed for stamina and others for building strength, always our instructors were with us doing the same.

If we went to the ranges to shoot within camp, we doubled [Ran in squads] if we went to D-lines area of the depot for SAA, we doubled, go to the lecture theatre if in lightweight trousers, shirt tie and jumper combination of rapid march and double. Go to lunch march. The official PT was initially carried out in lightweight trousers, a PT vest sometimes with a combat jacket over the top but always in boots DMS.

The concept of wearing training shoes was way in the future, I think it was only in circa 1988 that training shoes were issued in the Army IIi Tech as opposed to what were issued for the gym which we referred to as pumps electric or plimsoles that are the same as we had as school children they were made of mostly rubber and being black and having a toe cap that could be polished and of course we did so.

We initially started off with running in squads with a PTI or several, most of the time out through the depot onto the training area or onto the local roads around Pirbright. The runs would progress in distance and work up across the year to being undertaken in Skellington order webbing no rifles through to Full CEFO helmet and full complement of ammunition. It was called being fit to fight!

The army has or had two basic fitness tests when I served, the first was called the BFT or basic fitness test. It was designed as the minimum standard expected of every soldier from front line infantryman to office-based staff such as pay corps, chefs, mechanics. I think I am correct, but the test was in lightweight trousers, boots & pt vest.

The test started running and marching as a squad for 1.5 miles in under 15 minutes. At the end of that you dispersed as a group lined up like long distance runners on a track and after 30 seconds break the PTI said go and you did the return 1.5 miles back as an individual, however the time was reduced to 11 minutes 30 seconds. This was so easy in the depot but as you got older in the Battalion at times it could prove a struggle, I have seen Sgts Mess members turn up for the test after they had been at a mess function still half drunk and struggle through it, we were very fit alcoholics.

The other test is called the CFT or combat fitness test, for this you were basically in full CEFO kit weighing I think for us it was circa 25Lbs with rifle etc. It was a combination of running and marching at a hellish pace for 8 miles in just short of 2 hours which works out at 15 minutes a mile. At the completion of this you had to carry another Guardsman over your shoulder 100m, swap and you would then be carried a 100m to the back of an army truck and climb about without using the rope that is normally used to assist, then jump back down to the ground.

We would practice on the assault course in basic kit such as combat trousers PT vest and combat jacket learning the various techniques of how to get over each obstacle as an individual or if required as a group, we worked our way up to doing so from skeleton order without weapons through to full CEFO the most part practicing for the march and shoot that must be completed by everyone before passing out the depot.

We did log runs with eight to each telecom pole for endless miles though the surrounding woods near the ranges up and down the sandhill as punishment if we had not worked hard enough. The sandhill is as the name suggests a sandy hill.

I remember at one time some years later watching a film with my grandfather, he had been a WOII in the Essex Regiment, moreover, had fought in Burma during WWII as part of the West African Frontier Force. The film was called "The Hill" starring Sean Connery, Roy Kinnear and Michael Redgrave. In any case, I said to him that going up the sand hill was like the ultimate punishment being used in the film and that for us it was part of training, to which he said, "Good God!"

We started in the gym doing various circuit training rotations in our short's chariots of fire and plimsoles! We worked up to the test we had to complete such as throwing a medicine ball a certain distance and the one I dreaded climbing up a loose rope about 3 meters high and touch the cross bar holding the rope at the top, you then came down, the requirement to pass was to do this once. I for the love of money could not do this no matter how hard I tried, to do this required a technique of using your feet as a sort of break that held the rope still and you could pull you self-up after loosening your feet clamp them again like a concertina work your way up. The PTIs made it look so simply and no amount of screaming at me could I get it. In the end I used to with sheer force literally just try and pull myself up with my arms, and always fail.

I was on leave and watched the event no longer carried out called the Royal tournament, the navy sent teams of sailors from various ships to move a historic cannon, artillery piece and waggon across obstacles, It was gripping stuff, I noticed when using the ropes they kept their legs straight out horizontal when climbing or using them. I tried this when we got back from leave and it really helped, but I could still not do it, it was the same with the chin ups on the bar I could get the required amount done but it was not easy my upper body strength was just not that good. On the day of the tests that you must pass to get out of the depot I was as it stood on an anticipated failure due to the rope climb.

It came to my turn on the rope climb and with several "come on kipper" calls for encouragement I tried, failed and given another chance, the thoughts of being back squadded after all these months was too much and I jumped up bent my legs as I had seen the Royal navy do and with sheer effort got to the top touched the bar, but with the amount of reliance on my stomach muscles and bent legs I completely shit myself at the top, as I came down loose motion running and dripping onto the floor of the gym like someone bleeding, after a good kicking from the PTI towards the gym showers, accompanied by hysterical laughing by all left behind I cleaned myself up and was given a spare pair of shorts to finish. I remember Sgt McM smiling at me outside and saying, "I try hard Fish".

We also had inter-company boxing in the depot and were required to go into D-lines gym and do what is called milling against each other looking to find people for the boxing team. The idea was to find someone of your own size and weight and then with boxing gloves that must have been 50 years old start slugging away at each other. I had O.I and we had a brief discussion on not hitting each when waiting out turn too hard and to just get through it realistically and not get picked.

The instructors were on to this, and we were all threatened with all the hell the devil himself could muster if they thought you were doing so.

On our turn we minced round each other like some sort of Laurel and Hardy sketch until an instructor stood up and walked towards us and bang, O.I really stuck one on me and I stumbled back dazed, this then turned out into a windmilling arm swinging session with both of us exhausted at the end of the two minutes and thankfully told to sit down. I did learn to fight but taught on the job if you like by the old sweats, [Old soldiers] in the Battalion on the street of Croydon, again in the bars in Fallingbostal Germany fighting, [we always won] with soldiers from other regiments.

The fitness training was in the end very tough, but all geared towards that final term in the 12 months at the depot to pass the BFT, CFT, Gym, March and shoot etc as you could not get out of the depot until passed.

Chapter IX

Platoon Commanders week Scotland.

I am not sure why, but I think the reason for us having a thing called the platoon commanders week was due to our age. In later years I realised that as we were just 16, we were in fact training along the same timelines as that of a 6th form college. In addition, we had our long weekends and leave periods the same as college students.

I think with all the pressure we were under, the Army, or possibly just the Guards had this initiative in the yearlong training programme. I think in their own way the Army understood that some fun time was important in our development, that's the only reason I think off why we went to Scotland as no military achievements I can see came from it,

And so, for fun and frolics we headed to Scotland for our week of fun. I have heard some platoons went to France, but we headed to a place called the Guards hut Folder near Perth.

We travelled by train under the usual pain of death threats if we in any way misbehaved. We had our weekly fiver spending money, moreover the whole fiver as no boot polish etcetera was needed. The first obvious target was the train buffet and beer. I for one also agreed with a few others in vocalising that I knew very little about Scotland other than it was hilly and cold, and if anyone tried to get beer or anything resulting in me or us having to run around mountains in fuck all but pants and flip flops would be in for it as we all knew we would all have suffered not just the individual mis behaving.

It took hours to get to Perth, then to add more agony we went from Perth to Folder by 4 tonne truck. As far as I was concerned, I had the same foreboding as that when we went to Thetford albeit here it was quite different, it was barren country no trees, hilly to start, then gradually the further we went the more mountainous it became.

The main two-way road fell away, and we continued weaving our way via a single road until we turned into the driveway of the Hut or House.

It is common nowadays that we have things like TripAdvisor or Google reviews for such things as bed and breakfasts, chalet's, hotels, and holidays in general to get a feel for the accommodation and locale area. Thanks be to God, no such things exited back then, or I would have found some way to injure myself to prevent myself having to go.

After getting my bag I stood like all the rest in front of a whitewashed house that looked like it was ready for demolition, it was very cold and the wind swept over the mountain behind us with quite a force, hurriedly we all pushed our way into the briefing hut and put in groups of six. We were Shown where the kitchen was, outside lavatory and of course the sleeping hut lined with bunk beds two tiers high.

At dinner we lined up waiting for the 2 minutes, 2 minutes to start but it never did, the instructors were serving the food and joking about this and that whilst doing so. The food was hot and plenty of it. After diner we stayed in the dining room and was given our group and adult supervisor details as each day was laid out and each group would work in a round Robin of activities, there was hill walking ending in a camp site under canvas, a trip to a brewery, a day trip to Edinburgh for which we were to be given a 50% off entry ticket for the castle, there was pony trekking and canoeing. If you wanted, you could even go sea fishing instead of the brewery.

The evenings were to be relaxed and each group had to come up with some form of entertainment for the rest, all sounded good although not sure about the canoeing. My week as far as I can remember was Day 1 pony trekking, Day 2 trip to brewery, Day 3 Hill walking, Day 4 Admin, Day 5 Edinburgh, Day 6 cleaning and Day 7 return to Pirbright.

No matter what group you were in we were all rudely awakened every morning at 5:30 AM and ran circa a mile to the nearest entry to the nearest stream, stripped and ordered into the stream waist height and sing God save the Queen come out dressed and run back.

Breakfast was of course Porridge with Tea, toast, jam and marmalade, you made the toast yourself on the kitchen grill, good luck. My day horse trekking was pretty much uneventful apart from the fact that I was terrified, I've always been terrified of horses however they said to make friends with it. I shared my apple from my lunch bag upon meeting it.

However, as I walked up to it with all the assurances in the world, I had nothing to worry about after 10 minutes of trying to get onto it I realised I had the most vicious tempered horse in the pack. At one point when crossing a stream in linear formation i.e., one horse behind the other it bit the horse in front of me on the bottom very hard! at another point it managed to bend its head back so far it almost bit me on the lower leg.

I protested to the instructor and owners of the horse that I wanted a different horse but was told no. It was after lunch we went to mount the horses again for the return trip from nowhere the bloody thing managed to swerve its body round and give me a swift kick to the testicles, it took me almost 30 minutes to recover everyone waiting and moaning at me.

I refused point blank to ride the horse and instead I walked back with the people who own the horse pulling it along behind their own until it bit their horse, and the owner was thrown off, Ha! I was justified.

The one thing I can remember about being in the Hut was being starving at the end of each day and they must have known this as the amount of scoff they gave us was fantastic. In the evenings we had some form of entertainment only one night stands out in my mind and that was watching CG and HT both from Cornwall playing spoons; for those who've never seen this it's quite funny insomuch as the two people face each other across a table with wooden spoons clenched between their teeth. In turn one Leans forward and taps the other one atop the crown of the head with a wooden spoon. The opponent not in on the joke ask if the other can carry on and they swap except when the next person lowers there head instead of being hit on the head with a wooden spoon an unbeknown person behind them would hit them on the head with something far heavier such as a metal ladle from the kitchen.

It was made more and more funny as those who had that just happened to them became the audience for those being brought in one at a time from separate rooms to take part. We also learned songs that most Guards regiments share such as 'old king Cole was a buggar for his hole and a buggar for his hole was he, he sent for his wife in the middle of the night, and sent for his Guardsmen three' etc.

Moreover, learning the dance of the flaming arseholes for which you needed a long piece of toilet roll paper stripped out and one end made into a wick. The other end inserted in the anus cheeks and then set on fire whilst singing and doing some form of dancing.

'Get em down you Zulu Warrior, Get em down you Zulu Chief, Chief! Chief! Chief! Chief Ar-Delle zumba zumba zumba. Ar-Delle zumba zumba zay.'

The idea being to get to the end of the song before your arse burned. The other favourite was I am a music man I come from down your way, what can you play? to which you had to sing the reply 'I can play the big trombone, the big trombone' and imitate the action and sound. The next person asked had to wait for the big trombone then their instrument and on and on. It was I suppose Character building stuff, funny enough those still pissed after the brewery trip were the most enthusiastic.

It goes without saying we got very drunk on the freebees or tasters from the Whiskey brewery trip. I remember trekking on foot and camping out was uneventful LSgt/ T reminding us that civvies paid a lot of money to do what we were doing!

The canoeing was in old Army canoes well passed there sell by date however the lake we went to was stunning if only it had been warm! we learnt capsize drills and formation canoeing, took a stream that ran out from the lake and down we went becoming faster but nothing so vicious at that seen in the Olympics sport. I thought as we were cold and wet an inevitable warm us up by running behind the Bedford truck was on the cards but mercifully not, we went back to the hut in it all the way.

In Edinburgh I think myself, TT and WD took advantage of the 50% of and went to the castle, we were banned from being in any pubs and especially one and I guessed as we saw later the instructors were in it getting pissed. After inspecting the Scottish troops on sentry, we were told to get out by one of their NCOs who must have twigged we were squaddies taking the piss out of them. A local told us of a café found near to where they used to hang people in a cobbled square, we found it and had egg, chips, and haggis, stayed there all afternoon as we had no money really for anything else. The day before going back to Pirbright was spent cleaning the kitchen, yard, rooms and camping equipment etc.

The next day headed back.

Chapter X

Adventure training Fremington Devon

The saying all work and no play makes jack a dull boy is very true. The recruitment posters for the military at the time along with the tv recruiting ads were always focused on rock climbing, abseiling, skiing snorkelling, canoeing always in the background a picture of the potential recruit with a new car with a pretty female on his arm.

We did have this when we went to the now closed adventure training camp in Fremington Devon. I have never been the sporting type except for Rugby at school and in the depot, so for me this was just going to be another painful experience in getting messed about only this time from rumours I had heard in rivers, hanging from cliffs on ropes and being a 100m below ground in total darkness oh the joy.

I think we travelled down on the train in civilian clothing being picked up in Bideford station by Bedford trucks. Fremington looked a pleasant enough place it seemed to me like Oulton broad near Lowestoft Suffolk. The camp was the type built during WWII I think it was used as a holding camp for the D Day landings, in any case was used by the Americans in some form or another I remember an instructor saying something like that.

Our accommodation was one room that held all of us it was the first time I had seen three tier bunk beds. We were broken down into activity groups with an activity rota, we learnt abseiling from the water tower in the camp then out some cliffs along the coast. We climbed up and abseiled back down. Our instructors were not with us they handed us over to the experts in that field each morning so I started to relax thinking this might be ok.

Every morning started at 05:00hrs for a run around the locale, on the way out of camp we would stop outside the cookhouse and shout good morning to the chef making our breakfast, I have no idea why, but it seemed to amuse the instructors. I think maybe the chef was like them on the booze all night and was suffering in the morning.

There was no 2 minutes! 2 minutes! either, we had packed lunches every day, a clay pigeon shoot, Mountain bike trail rides, Hill walking I think we went to Dartmoor for that with a night out in tents.

The worst was the pot holing, why I will ever know anyone does this for a hobby? I absolutely hated it, crawling through the smallest of gaps in green army overalls helmeted torch all the time being goaded to keep going ever deeper.

It was for me and a few others terrifying, the knowledge that if you got stuck or there was a collapse you were most likely going to die over a week or so through lack of water etc. At one point we had to go under water and push along a water filled tunnel holding your breath heart racing scrambling along in the dark desperate for the exit and up through the water to air, as I said I have no idea why anyone does it when they don't have too horrible.

After some time, you get to a clearing, a sort of cave within a cave and sit around the edges and all the lamps are turned off and were told to sit in silence. It was as we were told the first time any of us had been in 100% total darkness and silence. It was eerie you could not see your hand even a few centimetres from your face and I could hear the pulse of blood by my ears. It is then that the story's start of a group of explores in the 30s went missing down here never to be seen again, the local legend had it that a beast of some form had taken them to its lair. Oh, great as if the place was not spooky enough.

119

I always try to find the funny in the absurd in this place I could not, eventually after twisting our bodies through what looked like impossible gaps and small tunnels, we resurfaced to the open earth I have to say with very much relief. After removing all the equipment we were asked by the instructors, I think they were Royal Marines or an ex Royal Marine who handed out the lunch bags did we enjoy that? to a man we all lied! even though they were not our instructors we had learnt the hard lesson, if ever you are asked if you are cold? to say no, or are you ok? to always say yes. If anyone had said no, I hated it, I don't know they being Royal Marines they might have simply accepted it, but if our instructors had been there an answer in the negative may have resulted in us going back in the caves no torches and naked or something else equally horrible!

In the evenings we were surprisingly left alone to sit in the canteen in the camp, the instructors by all accounts in the local pub outside camp. To make our sad little lives even better the camp had a washing machine and dryer absolute luxury. One evening a plan was hatched to sneak out and get some chips from the local chip shop we had seen near camp on our return each day. I and others instinctively and vehemently argued against it if caught I did not want to even imagine the consequences and the dissenters, we got our way.

Outside the camp about a five-minute walk was the beach we had an afternoon to relax there swimming, all in all, a good place to visit in fact I did come back to Fremington camp many, many years later when an instructor with Southeast London Army cadet force the place had not changed.

Another activity was canoeing which I had done before in Scotland the only difference was here in Fremington you had to walk-through knee-high clinging estuary mud dragging the canoe behind to get to the freezing water.

The night before we came back, we had a platoon smoker which is basically a BBQ in camp, even being given a can of McEwan's export lager. I look back now with happy memories of that week, no flash cars or pretty girls on our arms but most of the recruiting poster ideals we did do. If I had never joined the Army, I would ever have done any of the things, we did there.

Chapter XII

Thetford map reading

We travelled to Thetford in the back of 4 tonne trucks; it seemed to take forever to travel from Pirbright to Thetford, as we approached inland from the main road, I instinctively knew we were close as only the Army could head towards such a bleak and desolate looking place in the middle of apparently nowhere.

As we approached the camp and entered my first thoughts were that it reminded me of a WWII prison of war camp, or worse still a Nazi concentration camp I'd seen in films when growing up. The accommodation was Nisan huts made from corrugated wriggly tin; this was used as a covering shaped in a half-moon over the small shoulder high brick base buildings.

As soon as the tail board of the 4-tonne truck was taken down the shouting started, "come on, move" "Out, Out OUT!" all the NCOs were pitching in on mass, I thought to myself was I after all at a Nazi concentration camp? The only things missing were barking Alsatian dogs straining at the lease front feet off the ground, instead of the English "quick, get a move on` to" down ten press ups" was German words such as "Macht schnell! Rouse" etc.

I thought here we fucking go, it's time to either laugh or succumb to this impending physical and mental pain. I decided to take it all in and try to laugh at the unfolding dramas to come try my best to block it all out mentally and just go along. It was supposed to be map reading not battle camp; I had expected it to be like this on battle camp from what TS had told me from Flanders II but not this on Map reading training camp. After gathering up all our equipment and many press ups by the

4-tonne truck we were as usual doubled at very fast speed towards the accommodation.

Inside and central was an old coal fire with a piped chimney that went straight up and through the roof, a coal bucket and small shovel sat beside it. On each side of the room were bunk beds, in some cases three beds high. I got the name of the camp from a camp map pinned on the main door it was called Stoney Bridge Camp.

The 5-star accommodation known as Thetford battle camp Stoney bridge.

Some images of Stoney bridge camp in STANTA

After a what to do in the event of a fire briefing and the punishment that would be mitred out to anyone hanging wet clothing etc either near, on, or inside the fire surround of the coal fire we set off at another rapid pace accompanied by high volumes of shouted abuse by the NCOs, towards Scoff.

Scoff was in another purpose built cook house of wriggly tin construction and sat about 12 at a sitting, in that case you waited outside for the next sitting with you mess tins, knife fork and spoon, or K.F.S, mess tins are square shaped containers made from steel or aluminium the largest about 7 inches long and 4 inches wide and about 3 inches deep the smaller of the two sits neatly inside each other, both have a thin shaped handle that folds back on the mess tin. After waiting for about 4 mins, you could hear all the screaming coming from inside the scoff house. "Out! Get Out! Times up, out! "And those diners exiting and running from the other end the cook house towards the swill cage, and under supervision of a Corporal who would then throw away any food left into the swill bins which consisted of old dustbins, and then the throng were hustled away back to the accommodation, after washing tins and KFS.

It was my groups turn, and after having your mess tins, KFS and hands checked for cleanliness you shuffled in and held your tin under the hot plate and without ceremony the food was slopped into your tin and you sensing the atmosphere sat at the first place you could sit as the Sgt in the dining hall had started shouting 5 minutes as we first entered and then would shout 4 minutes etc. It was now that I realised the true meaning of the term scoff it really kicked in with absolute clarity as I and others around me started to shovel for all you were worth the food into your mouth, some people were just sitting down as the shouts of "times up! Get out" started and we were pushed and hustled out the door as we had seen the last lot of beguiled diners, luckily for me I never ate pudding and so I was able as other were doing still shovel on the move spuds and other food into my mouth whilst heading towards the swill bin. I had got at least all the meat and the spuds down me before I was forced by looks that would kill to throw my vegetables etc away into the bin. We then as the others were shuffled away towards the next concrete enclosure where two steel containers were located on a wooden bench these had hot water in one and cold in the other, the purpose being to wash and rinse your mess tins and KFS.

In the evening we had one of the few sights I can remember of the platoon commander LT D gave a briefing of what the week would entail with what I distinctly remember being his crystal cut-glass public-school accent, basically for the first two days it would be classroom-based instruction in the mornings followed by afternoons putting what we had learned into practice in camp as much as possible, making route cards. We would then move into the open country and follow them, by day and by night. This would culminate at the end of the week by an escape and evasion exercise with a night out under bashers, this was a term that meant a temporary built sleeping area made from your poncho which was stretched and tied off to trees, if possible, this basically formed in effect a waterproof lean to.

The mornings were always that same when in camp reveille was blown at 05:30hrs and with customary shouting, kicking and general mayhem we were chased out of the rooms in the morning in lightweight trousers, boots, putties, belt, and PT vest colour as previously ordered. This depended on weather was covered by a combat jacket for PT. We would all parade at the MT yard and off we would go, Lt D leading on a run in three ranks ranging from a quick 3 miles to at one time over an hour and a half later we returned from what must have been at least 6 or 7 miles.

These runs were interspersed with battle PT without weapons, for example carrying another soldier of your own size and weight over your shoulder until Lt D or a L/Sgt shouted change, you then swapped. In addition to these waterproof ponchos were dished out and an improvised stretcher would be made by placing A N Other in it and six of us would have to grab a hold of the material three either side and again keep running until the word change was shouted. In the local village, there was a pub called the Dog and Partridge and if we were lucky the NCOs might head there for a beer in the evening, and we knew then that PT would be perhaps slightly easier in the morning as they would not hopefully be in the mood the next day.

In the evening, the camp had to have a Fire piquet and a guard at the gate armed with a pickaxe and a whistle. One morning well into the week RA was missing from his bed at reveille and a look around the room confirmed this and we when getting dressed at a rapid rate of knots discussed between us was where he could have gone? Had he as we thought gone absent without leave A.W.O.L.

The answer was soon clear, RA having now expended so much energy in PT and map reading exercises and not being able like the rest of us get the food down was starving and during the night he had been found rummaging through the swill bins for leftover food and taken to the guard room at the camp entrance. I remember seeing him smirk at me as we were running out the gate from within the entrance of the guardroom door; he was being screamed at by a throng of NCOs.

I did not know whether to laugh or feel sorry for him, however when we met him back in the room he just laughed and said that he at least got out of that mornings run, moreover that no charges were being levied as Lt D had explained that any regimental history researchers in the future would not understand a charge book heading "Found eating Swill!" He was simply bollocked and let off; such was the legend of RA.

One evening we were as usual rushing our food down and as the 3 minutes was shouted HL having been held up in the queue shoved a whole chicken leg or breast down his throat and started to choke, he was about three tables in front of me and stood up head moving up and down with a terrified look on his face and holding his throat with both hands panicking. Sgt R McM told him to sit down, but he then tried to step onto the table in his panic, realising he was serious Sgt R McM and another Corporal grabbed him and within seconds were carrying out the

Heimlich manoeuvre, it did not work and after several more attempts by the Corporal this time it this still did not work, they then turned him upside down with Sgt R McM holding one of his legs an A N Other holding the other leg the Corporal started kicking him in the back with the flat of his boot, eventually the chicken leg or breast flew out across the room to the relief of all the NCOs. It was not for us though as this drama had bought us valuable minutes to for once to finish our food! from then on, we all asked HL to do it again in the que for scoff.

The first part of map reading training was to learn how to fold a map correctly in a concertina, in addition the care of maps, next the definition of a map, that being, "A bird's eye view of a piece of ground from different heights such as 25.000 feet and has symbols and to represent items on the land below" or words to that effect.

It has been years since I lost my Guardsman's manual, but I remember the manual explained this very well I understood. The Guardsman's manual that we were all Issued with covered everything from drill to field craft to Skill at arms.

In the afternoon, we went by 4 tonne trucks to a range which had range points from 100m to 300m I was in L/Sgt TC squad for this training, and he was a very good instructor not really a drill and classroom person more a field soldier, he made us all walk at a steady pace from the firing point towards the 100m target lane and told us to remember how many paces we had taken.

On our return to the firing point, he explained that the grid squares we had seen in the classroom on the maps were approx. 1 KM square and that 10 x 100m made a KM, it necessarily follows that if we walked 1000 steps, we had walked a thousand meters or 1 KM. It made sense to us all he then made us do an exercise called "Squad average", which is more field craft training but as he explained relevant to today's lesson. He asked each of us, and there were eight; how far we thought an object was in the distance bearing in mind we had just walked a 100m.

I do not remember what everyone's answer was today but the principle was that each person gave an opinion, you then totalled up the answers from all for example solider A 150m, solider B 170, C 200, D 250, E 200, F 150, G 170, H 220, = 1410 you then divide that by the number of Soldiers guessing i.e. 8 round that figure up or down and that should be the distance to that point, in this example it would be 175M. However, life is made much simpler if you only use four soldiers as the maths is simpler and not everyone strong point, the first four A, B, C & D coming at 190 M, not that dissimilar.

We tried this method and walked towards several pre-known points measured by the instructor prior to training by trial and testing that I for one trusted this method as accurate. We also used to bracket a method by which you knew what a 100m was as you had walked it so often and shot on ranges at 100m that you simply overlaid a 100m over and over a stretch of ground in your mind's eye towards the target and from that made an educated guess.

We learned how to make route cards in the classroom from maps, then putting them into practice on the ground setting of in twos time elapsed in between groups so that we simply did not follow each other, we learned what magnetic variation was and how to appreciate that into maps bearings, we used compasses to march onto bearings and how to dog leg around objects.

Lt D was particularly good at teaching and when it came to things, I struggled with he was very patient and would separate the Mongs as Corporal MG would call us and go through it again. It was not all screaming and shouting, I think if it was most of us would not have learned I for one would have simply switched off and head down until it was over that was what Lt D and L/Sgt TC were very good at taking time and patience.

The map reading training culminated in the escape and evasion exercise, it is necessary to point out that we were not the only training Guardsmen in the camp, others were actually on their battle camp training and it was good to see what lay ahead of us and it did not look pleasant, however, to make this training effective a regular set of fully trained Guardsmen and NCOs from any one of the Guards regiments were stationed in the camp to act as the enemy for section attacks etc, they were collectively known as the "Demonstration Squad, or demo squad for short.

It was on this camp we learnt that a 4 Tonne truck was a luxury we learnt the military skill of running behind trucks. After our lesson in the morning with L/Sgt TC about judging distance on the range the 4 Tonne would turn up but the NCOs would find fault in the squad or A.N Other and as a punishment would line us up in three ranks, behind the truck which would head of in front of us by about a hundred meters or so tail board down, we would then run in three ranks wearing full CEFO without weapons all the time instructors shouting A.N Other who might be struggling did they want them to stop the truck? Of course, we all knew to say yes meant you would be back at the depot and home with mum and dad within the next week or so. They played mental games with you.

We went to a range behind our truck one of the training days to test our head for heights, its aptly called the confidence course. It was a rope course high in the trees If I remember at least 25m high in places running the length of the woods the idea being to conquer your fears, by completing the course unaided by anyone. It was very frightening, and any fall was probably going to cause severe injury or worse.

In any case there was nowhere to go except up or get sent home! I was ok after I accepted that fact but at one point there is a gap about a metre between two trees circa 25M up that you had to climb a foot or more onto a wooden platform only a boot width like a scaffold plank, the only way across was to jump the gap. It was a case if you did not get a grip of yourself and just do it you never would.

I remember one member of the platoon froze and no matter how much shouting of encouragement from the ground he would not move until Sgt R McM gave him several seconds to get on with it or he would come up and throw him across. This threat did not work and unbelievably starting up the course went Sgt R McM the frozen J/Gdsm all the time watching as he got closer and closer and when he was a few feet away, lo and behold he jumped across, much to the cheering from below. It was a great motivator the temper of Sgt R McM. I am aware as I type this that many ex Coldstreamers will have by now worked out who Sgt R McM is and will know he was not a bully, he just got the best out of you. He did not suffer fools or the idle and never ever asked you to do anything he would not do himself, and when he got to the top of those trees without a second hesitation jumped across the gap.

[An interjection, later in my military career aged about 25 I went on a NCOs course, a promotion course as I needed more money. The Officer in charge was former Sgt R McM however by that date he was either the rank of RQMS or a Major I really can't remember, any way he was in charge of the course.

132

I was made by one of the instructors to run up a very, very high hill atop of which was the firing range red flag on a pole. He sent me up to put a 20 Litre water jerry can by the flagpole as he thought with it being dry a fire could start and spread.

However, he had a caveat that after almost 7 weeks of being on the promotion course he told me I had to run up and if I walked once, he would fail me on the entire course.

I went up and when I got back down, he sent me with another jerry can, again off I went and when I got back down, said he thought the last jerry can was not a full one and to take another.

I did and when I got back down anyone looking at me could see I was exhausted & ready to collapse, but I had never walked once.

He knew that and said he changed his mind and wanted to swap the first can for another one, I picked it up and was on my way when Major R McM called me back and said to join the firing line on the range and commented to the Instructor he was wasting his time as he knew me well as I was a junior Gdsm in his platoon at the depot and was known to him as "I try hard Fish" and that I would die on that hill before walking loud enough for me to hear.]

The week culminated in the escape and evasion phase, in essence we had green army overalls on, a sleeping bag, a poncho one water bottle between two and a basic map we had made ourselves, we were split into groups of 6, we had a 24 hour ration pack between two and if we wanted another one we had to make it to a meeting point by 7am the next day as a friendly comrade from the civilian population would supply us and they would also give us new bearings towards the pickup point for 7am the following day and from there we would get transport out of the enemy area back to our own lines.

It sounded simple enough, the demo squad and instructors were the pursuers and by all accounts if caught it might get nasty. The game was up we soon realised when making our maps, it dawned on us that factors stacked against us was the boundaries that we were to keep within. In the south running from East to West which was a main road that we could not go beyond in addition it was this road we were to go to if anything went wrong as a landrover would regularly drive along for that purpose i.e. safety In the north again running from East to West almost parallel was thick tree lines with open fields between e. g fire breaks with almost also running again parallel was a power line. This also restricted us from moving from above that line so we were basically narrowed into one small strip of land or corridor that we could traverse through from point to point, it was a bit unfair.

However, we were where we were and set off from the back of the truck at the drop off point moving quickly on the on the bearings from our home handmade maps, we had not got more than five or 600 metres we decided to have a group discussion in a hedge row we decided to stop there and watched as the truck pulled away. The idea was to stop here and simply hide, not move all day until the evening that way we could take the advantage of not being seen in daylight. Looking for us would be of course the demo squad and the instructors who had night vision equipment such as the IWS and had placed themselves pretty much across the whole route that any of us would likely have to take.

We moved off at about 10pm and decided to move all night towards the civilian meeting point a range hut however by about 12:30 we were caught, the instructor took from us six items from the ration pack. And then let us on our way not sure why he did this, but it led to an argument between us all what we can what we should now eat. we split the biscuits and head off no surprise we were captured again about an hour later and more food was taken from us we were left I distinctly remember with only a pack of spangles between six of us.

Morale was on the floor, and we decided after an argument to split up and head out in twos as being in threes was far too obvious for anyone viewing us on night vision. Myself and I am sure DS from Sussex spotted lights in the distance from a farm building, being either lazy or tired we cut across the middle of the field rather than going around the edges taking cover from within the hedgerows sure enough we were caught this time it was by the demo squad and we got a severe kicking they took away the laces from our boots stripped us of our overalls and sleeping bag leaving us only with pants and our ponchos.

We then moved demoralised towards the edge of the field and stopped for a rest after going extremely slowly from dip to dip in the hedgerow to the next keeping as low as possible to the ground, eventually the sun was coming up and the rays were coming through the hedgerow trees. We both decided to sit as trained with our own stand to and listen, we could hear the distinct sound of the Land Rover tyres on the road about 200 or 300 meters away as it went by, I suppose doing the job as described.

We were starving the farm building we had hoped to get to a few hours earlier was only 500 or so meters away and we decided to head closer and look thinking we could stay there all day somewhere warm and there might even be some water. We got to the farm and hid in the barn which had potatoes hidden under straw which was a bit odd? DS made me laugh saying, "only fucking carrot crunchers could hide spuds like normal people would hide money" he of course knowing I was from Norfolk! anyway we settled into a corner and started to eat the spuds raw! We looked a sorry state both our faces filthy with bloodied scratch marks from hedgerow brambles both arms and lower legs in a similar state, I had on white pants that looked filthy. We wrapped our ponchos around ourselves and decided to sleep.

I was woken by the sting of something across my thighs which had become exposed from under the poncho sometime later with heart racing and through glazed eyes It became clear the farmer had found us and had hit me with a garden cane. I think he was as scared as we were. I was personally in no mood and asked him in not so nice language what his problem was he then Ponting to the ¾ eaten potatoes at our feet.

After a brief exchange he told us to calm down and to stay put he would make us a hot drink and bring it out to us with some toast. The very thought had us both in a new found good mood, he was gone quite some time and before we knew it the Land Rover pulled into the yard and we were frog marched by the driver and passenger to the drinking trough for cattle and thrown in one after the other, thoroughly soaked herded into the back of the landrover much to the amusement of the farmer who had obviously reported us to the local military.

Bastard.

I swore to myself one day I would return and give him a punch on the nose! the landrover driver and passenger took us to the side of the road and gave us both a kick in the back side when getting out the back of the vehicle telling us if we got caught again we would be stripped of our pants, I did again think to myself what is it with me and underpants and the military.

We headed of towards the next point with no map just heading what felt correct as we had no maps and no compass by this stage just keeping the road to our right, eventually we could see other groups doing the same no wonder we were all being caught. On the odd occasion members of the public would see us sitting in the hedgerow I can only imagine what they must have thought we naked all but a poncho and boots with no laces each time we realised we had been spotted we quickly moved on in case they dobbed us in.

When evening came DS and I resolved to simply lay down on the reverse slope of this field and sleep, buggar it trying to get to the end point. However, about 2am the cows came in I imagine from another field and out of curiosity wandered around us shitting everywhere perhaps a nervous reaction to us and marking their territory I was scared stiff all DS could say was "Kipper do you know how to milk one of these!"

We moved into the waterlogged ditch too tired to care anymore trying to sleep with a trillion midges biting us everywhere. At first light we headed for the road and after about thirty minutes along came the Bedford truck, stopped and we clambered aboard to find most of the platoon inside looking as dishevelled as us, how miserable, I made my mind up then if I was ever in any kind of war and taken prisoner as long as I was dry had a bed of sorts and some type of grub I would stay and not try to escape sod all the public school boy nonsense like I had seen in Colditz.

We travelled up and down the road picking up like minded members of the platoon one I will not say who, had shat himself, he had a bad grumbling stomach from drinking from a stream if I remember he stunk to high heaven and was the reason that what happened next back at camp happened, we were all stripped of poncho boots in the MT yard and without any concern hosed down with the Fire hose freezing.

From there we went to the rooms which now looked like a five-star hotel got dry clothing on and down to the cook house for breakfast, however there was no shouting of 2 Minutes! 2 minutes! We did not need it; we attacked the hot food like Zombies it was eaten well under the normally given time!

All the equipment was checked cleaned and handed back, we had a hot shower shave and packed ready for the train back to Pirbright, I remember looking at the civilians in the station who were looking at us and thinking what do you know about anything?

Thetford battle camp

Chapter XIII

As we pulled into the camp my heart sank remembering our last visit here doing map reading some months before. In Thetford Battle camp the primary role was to teach us battlefield skills and survival. The battlefield skills are broken down into different stages, to the best of my recollection they started from where the Bedford truck dropped us off and moving in various patrol formations across fields and woods carrying full battle kit no large packs left on the truck as these would be brought to us later, we patrolled to a predesignated defence area where we would spend the next four nights in what was called routine in defence. The idea was that we were part of a company in defence. This involved setting up two man and three-man trenches in a circular fashion, like that you see in the films of the Wild West the Indians would ride around the prospectors in their circled waggons. The three-man trenches were for the gun team of which I was a part with RA and SO.

This machine gun needed three men to use it because of the weight and all the ammunition. The GPMG or general-purpose machine gun or affectionally called the Gympie it was manned by three Guardsmen was the best weapon in the platoon for what's called sustained or suppressed live fire. It is an excellent defensive weapon, and the instructors explained the best place to position the gun for best defence. The gun was the same calibre as our rifles and each man in the platoon carried at least 200 rounds of ammunition for the gun. The gun could fire at a much faster rate and spread the bullets in a wide pattern that could take down enemy who were attacking in greater numbers. The only issue was that after constant fire the barrel had to be changed as it would overheat, and the gun would often jam. The only other weapon as heavy as it was the 84MM Carl Gustav anti-tank weapon. We carried everything exactly as it would be in battle full section weapon including 66 mm anti-tank weapons filled with sand to stand for the weight fully loaded. We laid belly down in circles in our sections each man having his right leg over the left calf muscle of the man opposite to him this way we had all round defence fire, and we could communicate with each other by not having to speak. If a message had to be given, then it could be given verbally and quietly due the proximity if we needed to move or other messages such as move out and continue patrol, we would have a set of signals pre rehearsed as part of our SOPs. This is a set of instructions that are used universally by everybody and fully understood down to section level for example tapping three times on the persons next to your leg meant we were moving off and when the three taps on your other leg came back you stood up and set off in single file to continue the patrol.

We went into all round defence in our sections and section by section moved off to form the full defence position, one section North, two section East, three section West, and four section South with Platoon headquarters in the centre. The gun team would always be located facing the most likely direction of the enemy approaches or known direction from which it was expected to attack. We made range cards particular to each trench with known reference points such as corner of wood 500 meters with vertical sticks in the ground to mark your specific arc of fire. In addition, there was a location for the gas sentry who would be further out from the main defence position whose duty was to lookout for smoke mist or anything that could be a possible gas attack. The sentry would have two metal objects such as one magazine bashing against another or two mess tins or any metal-to-metal bashing

140

at the same time shouting gas, gas, gas over and over so the rest of the defence position would then put on nuclear biological and chemical warfare kit.

Once we had been found on the ground where an instructor had marked out where our trench should and the others, we began digging in our gun trench. They are normally circa 6-foot-long 5 ft deep as a two-man trench with an extra two foot for the sleeping or bunker. Our Gun trench would be it was 7-foot-long including in this length was another foot for the sleeping or bunker. Its purpose was for artillery cover. As we had three in the gun trench, we would have two men digging whilst one man on his belly rifle facing outwards toward the likely approach of the enemy protecting the two-digging in.

Obviously, we changed roles every hour until the trench was dug. We were told it should not take more than four hours to dig in and rivetted the fire trench and sleeping covered bunker. We were digging in Thetford training area and the ground after two feet became very chalky and difficult to dig it became obvious, we were not going to complete this in four hours. However, the instructors didn't care, we would dig until they were completed. This obviously meant that we were digging throughout the night. What we did not know was about how many more times we were going to be messed about throughout the evening. At sundown we did a thing called Stand to, this is where everybody puts on full kit gets into the trench rifle facing outwards and stand still waiting for an enemy attack until it's fully dark.

Once Stand two was over we were told food would arrive in metal containers, it became obvious after a while that the food was not going to come. It goes without saying, no one had the nerve to ask where the food was as that would be what the instructors wanted. Eventually the word went around from the instructors that unfortunately due to our defence position not being properly built at least an hour before stand to it was unsafe for the food to be delivered by the quartermaster in his lorry.

The redeeming feature was that if all was complete by first light and stand to, in addition the defence position was up and running, we would get hot water for washing and a hot breakfast. Sadly, throughout the night we had several times to stand to, these were several fake attacks by flares sent skywards by persons unknown simulating attacks such as gas attacks, when this happened, we would have to stop everything we were doing Gas mask on and change, getting into NBC equipment.

Thankfully, this was done at night-time because I had forgotten to bring my gas mask and there is no way I would have ever admitted it, I foolishly believed I could get through battle camp with no Gas mask. As it was night no one noticing I simply covered my face by pulling the hood draw cord tight.

The other thing I had forgotten was my large pack carrying my sleeping bag spare boots and other kit. I used my sausage bag instead. It's called that due to its shape which is like a boxer's practice or punch bag. I had chucked this on to the 4-tonne truck in Pirbright. The large packs arrived after stand to , but lo and behold any of us if we were to ask how come this can arrive but not the food? we dug all night and I distinctly remember it poured down around 3:00 o'clock in the morning, all the instructors we're walking around the trenches making sure we were still digging very selfishly I moved 20 meters or so with RA and hid in a dense tree line and caught some sleep leaving SO trying to explain where we were. At best we caught about 30 minutes sleep, however it felt like hours when we returned to the trench SO would not speak to us.

At daybreak we stood to everyone extremely tired cold wet and hungry, the mud around our trenches was now thick it would stick to the inner sole of the boots we stood down and the breakfast truck arrived. We were like madmen frothing at the mouth we could all be seen ripping open our large packs in my case sausage bag for our mess tins.

It was explained that one man from each trench would collect the food for the other from the central admin area, return and whilst one man kept on duty full kit facing the enemy the other would eat and vice versa, the food wasn't however dished up in our mess tins the instruction was to collect it in the tin helmet. It was dished up for both men in one helmet with the central helmet comfort provider removed.

The breakfast had everything in the helmet, tea, milk bacon, scrambled egg, beans, tomatoes, cornflakes, milk, for two Guardsmen, in our case for three, SO returned helmet full of food as he sat down to eat one of the training staff came over to our section and told us to stand to ! stand to as suspected enemy we're moving towards us, poor old SO was made to put the helmet on immediately minus the central comforter, this he did much to the amusement of the instructor and stood to with the gun. Both RA and I found it difficult to not laugh at SO with a streak of bacon coming from under his helmet resting on his ear.

The scene was quite surreal looking at those who had no choice but to put their breakfast all over their heads. No sooner had we taken position then they would say false alarm and expect us to continue digging. RA as always was starving hungry but now he was particularly starving for real on this occasion having used all the energy digging all the afternoon before and all night with no dinner, no breakfast he simply picked the contents off the floor wipe the mud off it and ate it.

I confess I wanted to do the same; by mid-morning the platoon Sgt R McM drove into the centre admin area with a Land Rover pulling a trailer full of kit. He explained to all that when your trench was deep enough and wide enough for you to stand in it with your webbing on and lean your rifle over the firing parapet you would be called over to the instructors who would then teach you how to cover the sleeping or bunker area off the trench.

This equipment I think it was called an IPK pack came in a small pack not much bigger than in an A4 envelope Inside was a large green sheet about 6 feet by 4 feet included we're metalled pegs sharpened at one end and a hole at the other, in addition to this was a long length of green cord or string. We were given two kits as our sleeping bay was bigger as there was three of us in this trench the instructor called us all over to the first trench qualifying for the construction of the sleeping or bunker. Sgt R McM explained to everybody in the circle around him the importance of constructing the sleeping or bunker part of the trench as things were no different to World War Two and that artillery could penetrate many bunkers, however this modern material we had been given was more effective then logs Wrigley tin covered by sandbags if built correctly, he sternly warned us this was hard work and required a degree of accuracy, he therefore instructed us to watch carefully whilst two of the instructors took us all to the first qualifying two man trench to watch how it is constructed. In essence you picked out about a metre beyond the hole in a web shape with the pegs and then run the string like a spider's web in a certain pattern through the peg holes. Then take the material place it over the edge of the material like you would sand on the beach to stop the draught coming under the wind break you would then have to slowly but surely increase the mud or dirt on the outside until it was about two feet thick then you would very carefully stop and start filling the centre over the hole, you always started at the outside increasing the weight there working inwards until you had the bunker at least two feet thick in mud in the centre. Then re turf over the top and the firing parapet and try to make the fire trench camouflaged. When the demonstration of how to do, this was completed taking about 40 minutes the two instructors put on their equipment and went and sat inside the bunker or sleeping bay pulling down the gas flap at the entrance.

We were told to move away from the trench and Sgt R McM went over to the Land Rover with trailer started the engine and drove towards the two man sleeping bay or bunker driving over it with the full weight of the Land Rover and trailer turning around and driving back again over the two men sleeping area much to my horror It dawned on me that they were going to do this to us! with a certain amount of trepidation we were told we would have the same amount of time to do this we the gun team and the three man 84 millimetre trench could have an hour.

We went back to our trenches and continued digging until lunchtime wholly expecting that lunch would arrive soon in the containers, another flare went up and we put on all our equipment expecting the imminent attack by the enemy only to stand down after 10 minutes but given the notice that information had been received at platoon HQ the food truck had been blown apart during the last attack having not made it to our location. To say RA was angry does not cut it. Shamefully with my usual sarcasm I told him that SR had put his breakfast in a bag and had it in his large pack a nano second later hearing this from me he went two trenches over to buy SR slops; SR protesting he had no food! Unbeknown to us RA had a very real fear of confined spaces, and he became increasingly worried about the sleeping bay and being a bit of a bully, he told SO he was at the far end when the time came to get in.

By early afternoon, all trenches that should only take 4 hours were done. I was immensely proud as I thought we had done a good job. The sleeping bunker looked like it might work as regularly we would go and stand on top of it one person at first, then two, then all three of us expecting at any moment to fall the five foot down into the trench, RA couldn't put enough mud on the outer edges of the sleeping bay area. It was about 3:00 o'clock in the afternoon we were all told to get into our sleeping bunkers L/Sgt CM with another instructor drove the land rover over each sleeping bunker, RA refused to go in and was being kicked and punched to get in the sleeping bay bunker from the fire trench, Sgt R McM came over with a rifle and threatened to shoot RA, but RA did not believe him until suddenly Sgt R McM turned the butt of the rifle and started gesturing it towards RA`s head forcing him into open part of the Fire trench, myself and SO quivering in the sleeping bunker, RA came in shaking and sat in front of me and reluctantly pulled down the gas cover.

The Land Rover drove over us once and on the second time the bloody sleeping bunker collapsed. RA got out, turned, and pulled me by my arms out but SO was buried, there was a massed scramble for everyone in the platoon to come over and help dig him out, within no time at all he was above ground everyone was jealous as they gave him a mug of hot coffee for the shock!

Amazingly the instructors did not seem fazed by this and told us to quickly rebuild the sleeping bunker. Another two-man trench was told to help us. We then went into routine of defence such as washing and shaving, one man watching another on guard.

The instructors coming up to us and questioning us about what we had learned thus far? RA said that Sgt R McM was insane to which he got a good kicking for being smart. We had a demonstration on how to challenge approaching people whilst on sentry or on your own counting in the patrol numbers and passwords etc we had practiced this in field craft back in the depot, but this was in the field.

It was around 4 pm we thought the evening meal must be coming soon but lo and behold right on Q flares suddenly went up and the instructors pulling ring pulls of smoke grenades throwing smoke all around the whole defence position. In addition, a thick mist from outside the defence position was seen by all floating towards us intermingled were men all dressed in black clad and balaclavas and gas masks walking towards who were also throwing smoke canisters. The gas century screaming this time not like any time before with terror in his voice was shouting gas, gas, GAS! and bashing an empty magazine on his rifle barrel.

Now being 16 years of age and seeing Sgt R McC, driving a Land Rover and fully loaded trailer over the sleeping bunkers with one of them collapsing, I thought in all seriousness this was real gas. I had a grandfather who had served in WW1 in the North Staffordshire regiment he won the MM, he was gassed and told me it was truly terrifying and at first all they had was a neckerchief which they used took keep peeing on and breathed through that until it dissipated.

In my desperate panic, realising that I had no gas mask I instinctively grabbed the general purpose machine gun by the carrying handle so as not to commit the ultimate crime and leave your weapon unattended I ran as fast as my legs would carry me about 5 to 600 metres away from the trench towards the open fields behind me absolutely sure in my

147

mind that I needed to put as much distance between me and this gas as humanly possible.

I could hear the Land Rover horn being constantly pushed down so I stopped turned around and was beckoned back to the defence position. I did not dare walk so ran back but I realised the GPMG seemed very light when I looked to my right hand all I had was the barrel which detaches from the gun when it gets to hot so that a new cold barrel can be inserted. Fuck.

When I arrived back in front of everybody Sgt R McM asked me what the fuck was I playing at? I managed to garble to him that I thought it was real gas and I had not brought my gas mask, he became very, very red in the face furious, he pushed me back and back on my feet until I fell over backwards, he then asked me where my gas mask was? I told him Pirbright that it was in my large pack which I had also forgotten to bring.

He became more than furious and asked me where my spare clothing was, and I told him I'd got what was in my sausage bag. He then dragged me to my feet and paraded me around the middle of the defence position my feet hardly touching the ground saying I was the kind of dickhead that would get them all killed, not only because I would be dead in minutes from gas leaving them undermanned but on top of this, I ran away with 90% of the Platoons firepower. He frogs marched me back to the gun trench and told me a suitable punishment would be found.

Thankfully the flare went up again and this time coming out of the woods towards our defence position was about 20 men in a variety of black overalls foreign looking helmets Kalashnikov rifles throwing smoke and firing randomly at us.

We realised these were blanks and ran to our defence position jumping in our trenches. We got the gun reassembled with the blank firing attachment barrel inserted the three of us got the gun going. It was a simulated attack conducted with what we now know to be called the demo squad, the demo squad at my battle camp were Irish Guards it was a role you could take as a volunteer in Battalion to go to Thetford to be the enemy for the training recruits.

At one stage it came to hand to hand fighting and I was rifle butted in my chest so hard I couldn't breathe and collapsed on the trench floor, RA is called lofty for a reason and was able to grab the rifle and pulled the guy to the ground and proceeded to smash the demo squad man who had rifle butted me with his helmet against his helmet until he was told to get off.

I knew from that moment on if we ever went to war for real, I wanted to be where RA was. Even SO was up and at them, he was hanging around the neck of one of the demo squads from behind wrapping his legs so tight around him he could barcly walk it was very funny.

A short while later it became clear by the shouting that someone was in the shit, it turned out to be A.N. Other who had been the gas sentry at the time of the attack, but the platoon commander Lt D had crawled up sneakily to the sentry position unfortunately, I'd like to say this now, we had all done it at some stage, fallen asleep on sentry.

It was now I realised why the person screaming gas, gas, gas sounded so desperate earlier, A.N. Other had been caught and knew what a world of pain and hurt he was now in. I remember we all got the gossip as the two Junior Guardsmen bringing round water replenishment in jerry cans told us, we were allowed a cup of water to drink from our cups there and then afterwards fill our water bottles, this happened quite often thankfully as the water helped the hunger pains which were rife.

Shortly before the evening stand to the sad sight of A.N. Other crawling up to each trench came into view. He was in full kit and had a large pack on filled with sand the shoulder straps obviously dug into his collar and underarms. He was crawling along and obviously in pain as he got to the front of each trench, he apologized for being weak and putting all our lives at risk. He then crawled to the next trench so on, and so on around each trench in the whole defence position.

I just thought Oh my God if that's his punishment for falling asleep on Gas sentry what must Sgt R McM have in store for me after my running away during the last gas attack?

By this time, we were all very tired and hungry they knew that so it was like music to our ears we could hear the lorry coming along the track road banging and bashing its way along. We were told we were going to eat the evening meal in sections rather than as individuals. This meant we went to the metal containers, which incidentally were nicknamed dixies, each half section first, we would walk along the food line in full battle kit but allowed only one mess tin.

Eating from containers called hay boxes heavy but kept the food hot photo is of Moore platoon courtesy of Brian Eager IG

Everything you were given to eat went in the single tin. When everyone in the half section had a full mess tin the instructor started shouting 2 minutes, 2 minutes and we knew exactly what to do and started stuffing the scoff down you as fast as you could swallow. When the 2 minutes ended, you were told to stop, wo betide you, if you tried to take another morsel of food. What was left you emptied into the bin liner the trained soldier had put on the front bumper of his truck for that purpose.

I used to look at them, the trained soldiers thinking they must feel sorry for us. No chance, as they had all been through it themselves before passing out and becoming Guardsmen themselves. It was then on the double back to the trench stand ready whilst another section went to scoff. Stand to was undertaken until the sun had gone down and everywhere was pitch black, I had the devil of a job trying to stay awake as the recent food had indeed made me very sleepy, I found you could cat nap as you could rest the rim of your tin helmet on the rear sight of your rifle and in the dark it looked like you were awake.

After stand to one man from each trench was taken to the Platoon HQ and given a 24-hour ration pack which meant we would be feeding ourselves from now on. We readily unpacked the box shoving the contents into the large pack or in my case sausage bag. The officer Lt D was doing the rounds sentries times were made known the communication wire rerolled out between trenches and sentries posted the sentry duty was to be carried out in our trench, the gun trench. Lt D came around and asked us questions such as, what was the password, what was it after midnight all this had been communicated in the section orders after stand to.

He asked who was in this trench our Gun trench I replied Fish, RA, and SO sir. He asked who had told us to dig our trench here? We replied the instructor had when we arrived, he said he did not like it where it was, he produced white mine tape, which is like the type of tape the police used at an incident to mark off no entry. I remember watching as he moved about 4 foot forward rolled out the tape in a line and said fill this trench in and dig another one here.

I fully understood from when we first joined and reminded by L/Sgt HK that we wanted to join and that they the army only wanted the best and that they, the army would do everything they could to make us leave particularly as this was the Guards and it mattered not if only three make it through training from 100, the three he emphasised would be the best of the bunch.

I realised at this time and moment that every instinct in my body was to throw my shovel on the ground and ask to go home but remembering what he had said I just kept quiet but boiling inside. I think everybody felt the same way RA said this was rubbish and you could tell he was seething angry.

Anyway, the officer hot footed it to the next trench and after a few minutes he delivered the same verdict on the location of their trench and either move them back or forward telling the occupants to fill it in and start again. The GPMG was moved to the left of the trench and the junior Guardsman on stag sentry duty was far enough away so as not to get covered in mud as me RA and SO started shovelling the soil and sticky mud back into the fire trench after about an hour we were all summoned to come to platoon headquarters, we sat on our tin helmets in a line with our notebooks out.

We were going to carry out a patrol, the patrol was a reconnaissance patrol which meant that we were going to go and check out something in this case a suspected enemy platoon location, in addition, confirm the strength of the enemy what weapons all sorts of details, each man was to carry Skellington order webbing only which is a lot lighter that full fighting webbing, we were all checked for anything that could rattle we all fired a test round in the air at the same time so that anyone listening could not estimate our number, needless to say lots of personal infantry skills to tedious to mention were employed

Not everyone had to go as the defence position still needed guarding and new trenches needing to be dug, one man from each section was selected and formed the recce patrol. I was picked for the patrol and about 9 pm we set off. We had practiced the patrol techniques required for the reconnaissance patrol for several hours that afternoon within the defence position, we had also attended the full briefing of reconnaissance patrol this always seemed to have the same pattern the platoon commander would give an overall briefing of the situation on a

153

very large scale and then the instructors would lay this down at our level or company level platoon or section, in this instance we were to do reconnaissance of the bridge across the river between ourselves and the enemy, we were to look at suitable positioning for an ambush on the opposite side of the river.

We left across open fields using all the techniques we had been taught I have to admit it all felt very professional and I had confidence in the way everything seems to have been thought about such as what to do on lights close one eye keep your night vision keep the patrol formations be quiet when in or on defence and after about two hours patrolling we came to the final RV or rendezvous point. We went in single file along the riverbank the instructor pointing to the ground where the person behind him was supposed to lay down looking across the river after what seemed an age being bitten to death my nits and fighting not only to stay awake also the hunger pains, not daring to open your water to take a drink.

It came down the line we were moving across the bridge to the other side we did this in single file at a crouching walk when we got to the other side the instructor pointed one person to go left one person to go right either side of the bridge and wait for further orders all this had been practised in the defence position sometime in the afternoon as well as the use of mocked up models, we observed some distance away a fire and vehicles with side lights on and the enemy not being particularly tactical.

The Sgt instructor came along and taped everybody twice on the right shoulder which meant move to the right side of the bridge following him. I was not in this number however those that did follow him we're gone for about 40 minutes and came back which was correctly challenged and the patrol re crossed the river formed up into our last rendezvous point when everybody was accounted for, we patrolled back to the defence position getting in about 3:30 in the morning.

We then had to go to between headquarters and repeat what we had seen such as numbers of weapons enemy morale vehicle types and anything else considered important. When the debriefing was over, we returned to our trenches when I arrived SO was digging, he was about halfway down, and I asked him where is RA? He said I have no idea just after you left, he opened his ration pack I'm pretty much he ate everything he buried the empty pack under this parapet, he went to the to the loo came back with SD and another they gathered their stuff and walked off. I've no doubt he had no idea were. I never thought anything more about it as I was just too tired and started to help SO dig the trench.

As first light approached the familiar word went round stand to, SO and I packed everything away and stood to after standing down we started one man washing and shaving while the other kept guard the Sgt instructor came round to see how we are and what progress we had made with our trench also asking where RA was? SO explained that he thought he was on a task with two others as they left towards the platoon headquarters about 10:00 PM last night.

The Sgt instructor stood up and walked back towards Platoon headquarters. After about 5 minutes the instructor came back and took SO with him to platoon headquarters. I had by this stage washed and shaved my face and went over to join the other trench taking my gun with me and stood guard while the others washed and shaved it was then I heard the rumour that three people were absent had left Thetford battle camp!

It dawned upon me RA must have been one of them I thought to myself well that's his career over where on earth would you go. I made myself a hot drink of tea and cooked some bacon grill and beans whilst at the other trench shortly after SO came back and we both continued digging the trench I asked SO what was going on he said RA and two others we're missing. At around 10:30 AM Sgt R McM came into the defence position in the Land Rover and after 10 or so minutes we were all called into platoon headquarters suspending the full tactical exercise. He also called me over and gave me a large pack he had found.

We were all asked if any of us had heard anything about a pre-planned move by anybody to leave the battle camp, the honest answer from everyone was no. The three of them had made a spur of the moment decision to leave.

We went back to our trenches and continued hard tactical routine in defence we were cleaning the gun continuing the digging in and camouflaging until around 11:00 AM. We all then went for a briefing on carrying out an ambush for the early hours of that evening we practised cut off groups, killing zones, routes in, roots out, actions on lights as we had done for the previous evening reconnaissance patrol.

A model was used to show the bridge the river the woods where the enemy had been seen and the best place to ambush them on the opposite bank of the river to our friendly forces area the patrol or ambush patrol was due to go out at 1:00 o'clock in the morning.

We returned to our trenches had our lunch from the 24-hour ration packs and continue digging the trenches if needed. The incentive was that if you had finished your trench and bunker sleeping area if one of you stood to the other could sleep. It was a heavenly sent 30 minutes that I eventually got.

About 17:00hrs a landrover came into the defence position and from the back came RA and the other two, I know their names, but I will not put them here. There was an almighty shouting match in the command tent outside the perimeter of the defence position was. A little later RA came back to the trench weapon in hand grinning, I asked where they had gone, and he said they had got some sleep in a ditch by the main road they had come across then thumbed a lift into Norwich!

He went on to tell us that about 11AM they were trying to get a breakfast from a café giving the promise to would send the money on when they got back to camp, of course being refused they went into the British Homes Store and started shoplifting Mars bars, Coke, & Crips between them. They thought they had got away with it but found themselves a few minutes later in a park mouthful of a Yorkie bar later surrounded by police.

It never occurred to them what they looked like in faces covered in camouflage cream wearing Nuclear Biological & Chemical Warfare suits. To this day I do not know why there was no more repercussions it was as though it never happened maybe the Guards old boy network at its best with BHS and the Police.

I could see from RAs face he was not sad he had gone least not as he said they got a meal from the police awaiting pick up!

With trench now finished we prepared for the ambush test firing in mass our weapons checking each other for rattling items etc re attending a briefing or section orders. At 01:00hrs we went out to the Ambush position conducting all the patrol formations and actions on it was really I thought very professional.

After laying up in the final rendezvous position just listening for a while we went across the river, I was halfway across the Baily bridge and heard a scream and splash which being the middle of the morning was louder than normal. A.N Other had got up and fell in. Immediately the enemy sent up flares and we had to run like hell back to the final RV get down in all round defence You could hear A, N Other sloshing his way back absolutely wet through.

I wanted to laugh but it would have been the end of me. After 20 mins or so we patrolled back to base to make the report on the ambush that never was, the only person getting any benefit from the training according to one Sgt was A.N. Other who was cleaner that the rest of us as he had a bath.

After the debrief we return to the trenches, as the patrol was recalled to our trench mates who had stayed back you could hear stifled sniggers and giggles coming from around the defence position.

We snatched sleep between stags and stood to as first light was looming, this was always about 04:30 or 05:00hrs and sure enough as soon as it was getting light enough to just about see the Sgts started throwing thunder flashes around by the bucket full.

A thunder flash looks like a stick of dynamite in the films, it was struck with a match and thrown to the floor making a very, very large bang, in front of us was several landrover coming across the open ground GPMGs firing and black clad soldiers about ten or twenty, they too were throwing thunder flashes.

We although startled fired a few rounds back but the Sgts were screaming bug out! BUG OUT! and so we put on large packs and started running backwards in our case towards a red filtered torch, soon enough we were in three ranks huffing and puffing for at least an hour until we stopped and were told we had to cross the river ahead of us.

We had practiced flotation packs back in Battle camp as a sort of side lesson, it meant stripping naked and putting everything except your weapon in the poncho with some sticks and wood to help it float. This was tied at the hood with the draw string. I am fully aware that every Guardsman you meet will tell you they had to break the ice in Thetford to do their river crossing, well we did. We queued up in line hidden by very high reeds swaying backwards and forwards taller than us, we looked a sight milk bottle white bodies with black arms necks and faces with an anticipated look in all the whites of our eyes.

I think for their behaviour RA and the other two were first in after breaking the ice with the rifle but, RA could not swim and we knew that from PT at the depot swimming pool, he was though assured it was not too deep and he had height on his side, across he went with the rope the 20 or so meters across tied the rope of I think to a tree and came back, the GMPG, Charlie G and the 66mm Rockct launchers were called for and the three of them a weapon each startcd across, the rest of us following in silence other than the ooooh arrrrrg as testicles went north again leaving the sack empty in protest.

Flotation packs

When we arrived on the other bank of the river no surprise, my kit was soaked including my last few remaining cigarettes, this took a huge toll on my morale, even though it was already on the floor as I stood shivering stark-naked tipping the water out of my boot like hot water out of a kettle.

The Sgts started hurrying us up to get dressed, I think dressing in wet clothing should be an Olympic sport, it's incredibly difficult as everything seems to stick to you. In any case we were soon in three ranks and doubled at a much faster pace than normal for about an hour you could see the steam coming of all of us.

We eventually arrived back by the river in an open area that had room for parking. We were given a ration pack and without any fuss we went into all round defence in the nearby woods and dug what are called two man and three-man shell scrapes. This is a defensive trench but not deep it has all the soil that has been dug out heaped at the head and we put ponchos over the top ties to trees for rain. We had breakfast one man watching whilst the other shaved and got the breakfast on for both of you. It was odd that we were left alone. A.N Other took the Communication wire around the position and sentries were posted we were by now well experienced in what we needed to do.

It was whilst we were doing this that a Bedford truck arrived and the trainee Grenadier platoon, Gibraltar one arrived, they headed to the woods near us and started the same. They looked filthy and dog tired, I realised we also looked the same all our eyes were blood shot red through lack of sleep.

After everything was as it should be the word went round "non tack" which meant things were relaxed a little. We were called to the riverbank where some flatbed green army boats were tied to the bank, we were going to learn watermanship skills in sections of eight.

We learnt how to carry the boat and lower in the water making no noise ensuring the stern was facing the way the current was going. When the boat had been secured or tied, we went into all round defence in the order we were going to get in. We would lay just listening for about 5 mins and then at the kick of the calf muscle went round and the first man went to hold the stern, the next to hold the bow so that the boat was length ways along the riverbank. Then the GPMG went in and laid prone with the gun facing the stern, then what was called tail end Charlie i.e., the man at the back went in facing the rear followed by the next four then the last two holding the boat got in. six in the middle did the rowing in unison across the river which was much wider than where we had done the river crossing hours earlier.

At the opposite bank of the river the two men who held the boat at the stern and bow left first followed by the GMPG who laid down facing the direction of the enemy the rest getting out tail end Charlie being the last in all round defence again waiting about five minutes just listening.

We went backwards and forwards crossing the river practicing each person taking a different role in the boat until we had it. The remainder of the platoon were improving shell scrapes and an allowance had been made to dry some kit in the trees.

The Grenadiers doing the same. It was then the fun and games started, the instructors decided to have a competition between us and the Grenadiers, basically in teams of 16 twice the capacity of the boats were to strip down to underpants only, then from a position on land the word go run! Was shouted and everyone picked up the boat and run with it to the river.

A points sheet was created with a starting number and points would be lost if anyone talked, anyone fell over, anyone falling in the river, and the time to get to the other bank then take the boat out of the river to another team on the opposite bank of equal number they did the return trip.

Everyone ended up in the river at some stage and one boat sank not to the bottom but was floating full of water having to be pulled out by rope.

We packed the Boats away and went back to the all-round defence position. We were told lunch was being delivered by Bedford truck and all we needed was KFS and a mess tin, I for one and I guess everyone else I suppose did not get too excited by the prospect of a hot meal as I'm sure they would find a way out it.

After speaking to some Grenadiers, they had the same issues and we had realised then that the flares going up at lunch time in the distance roughly the same time as us was them getting the same treatment!

What happened next was very strange we were told to get in groups of three and each group of three came out in front of all assembled Grenadiers inclusive and each group to show its war face with screams. The Sergeants really getting us fired up, we having to shout Kill, Kill, Kill etc.

Then the truck arrived and one person from each group of three went forward to get the ration, which was in an empty sandbag, I collected ours the bag being tied at the top but the inside had something moving what on earth I thought as I walked back.

We were told not to open the bag after until everyone had collected them. Stepping out in front of us was a Grenadier Sergeant who told us we either had a chicken or rabbit for lunch and he was going to show us how to kill them, I thought to myself you must be fucking kidding!

Anyway, we were all called forward to the riverbank he stood and explained that taking a life was not something to be done lightly and if possible, it should always be done humanely and quickly.

He reached into the bag a took out the chicken, which was doing its best to get away, He eventually got the bird to his left-hand side against his hip with his left hand turned back slightly and holding the bird's legs in his hands, with the crook of his arm around the body like a bagpiper holds the bag pipes.

He then said you must wait until the bird has calmed down somewhat and when it had you then use your right hand making a ring around its neck just behind the head forefinger to thumb palm facing towards the direction the bird was looking. He then said you gently pull the next outwards until it would extent no more and then make violent quick upwards motion with the head at the same time pulling at the neck and it would break.

He then went onto show the other method which was to hold the bird by the feet with your left hand and wait until the bird settled down which it did and again making a ring with the thumb and forefinger pull the neck down gently as far as possible then with real force turn the birds head upwards again and pull at the same time.

He asked if anyone had any questions, someone pointed out he had a shovel on his webbing why not chop its head of with it. The answer was that this was messy as blood would go everywhere and there was no guarantee you would strike the neck and he for one would not trust anyone with a shovel not to chop his hand whilst holding the animal down. Moreover, you may just be on your own with no one to hold it down. It did make sense what he was saying, he then took the bird back under his arm as in the first lesson and within seconds the bird was dead. It kept flapping around and he said it should be left for a while as the blood will still be pumping. He put the dead bird by the riverbank.

Now it was time for the rabbit which was pretty much the same two methods as with the Chicken either holding it or dangling it by the legs the result was the same in either case a dead Rabbit.

He then took out a very sharp knife from his webbing and cut the head of the chicken to which several of the assembled started throwing up. He then cut of the claws or and the tips of the wings and laid it down for the blood to trickle into the river. He then did the same with the rabbit starting with the head and paws.

He returned to the chicken and said this was not for an enjoyable pot roast for a Sunday lunch with all the trimmings. I was pure protein to get us going from A to B. The bird would not therefore be plucked and left with the skin on it was to be skinned.

He put the tip of the knife blade where the throat had joined the head turned it sharp side up and push it along making a long cut, he did the same with the with the legs. He then moved to the edge of the river cut it open from the anus through the belly and breastbone, he pulled it open and tipped all the guts into the river.

He then washed the carcass in the river then stripped all the meat he could from the bones. He righty said this is all we needed and to boil it in a couple of mess tins after chopping it up into bite sized chunks. It was again a very similar method for the rabbit. He washed his blade in the river stood up and gave the meat to one of the instructors.

It was our turn now, what now ensued would have been recognised as a blood bath perfectly acceptable carried out by Genghis Khan. I for one in our group was not putting my hand in the sandbag as every time the three of us looked in the bag or tried it to get it out it would peck at your hand. We were rather pathetic and encouraged each other to get the bloody thing out of the bag. I stopped and looked around and what a scene, Sergeants were shouting and screaming at people.

A N Other was crying and shaking his head in defiance at being told to kill his lunch.

A N Other was running around screaming at the same time swinging the chicken by its neck around and around his head like a football scarf they had worked him up so much. The bird was shitting itself quite rightly and it was spraying everywhere.

A N Other was drowning their lunch in the river in the bag.

A N Other was swatting the bag at the tail board of the Bedford truck as though in a pillow fight.

Another group all three of them had their shovels and were basically beating the poor creature to death.

A N Other was running around with his two comrades chasing the bird which had escaped, to our left A N Other from our platoon who came from Devon had as calm as you like killed their Rabbit and he quickly walked over to us and before we knew it our Bird was also dead.

We moved down to the river and made a good attempt to skin our chicken as we had been shown, the issue we had was the knife we had was from a dining room as blunt as the end of a rubber pencil. In the end we resorted to just ripping the skin of with our fingers later using the edge of a shovel to open it to get the guts out.

I can tell you now with several oxtail soup sachets from our compo ration added to the water all three of us scoffed that chicken down it was like an adrenaline injection I felt the energy level in me surge like a Duracell toy.

The riverbank was a right mess, the river ran red with blood but after we had cleaned it up you would not have known we were there, we always left anywhere we went cleaner than we found it!

The rest of the afternoon we spent in groups away from the defence position to practice section attacks. The Sergeant teaching us knew we had already done this at the depot in field craft lessons and watching SKC films.

He could see we were on our chin straps and moved us to an area surrounded by high reeds and basically said he would watch for us and to get our heads down. It was many, many years later through social media that I reconnected with him, and I told him how much I respected him for allowing us that hours' sleep that day!

We returned and had the evening briefing, in essence the enemy had advanced and chased us back to the position we were at now, However the re enforcements i.e., the Grenadiers had arrived and that tomorrow we were going to a range to zero weapons and the advance to contact to move the enemy back behind the road they have settled behind. We had a brief as though we were the lead platoon of a company attack, this would be a live firing exercise and we would get the ammo etc at the range.

We passed the night with routine in defence sentries posted at each section staging on and trying to get some sleep as most of us had by now partially dried out sleeping bags, even so we managed about 3 hours throughout the night. The reason being every time a bloody flare went up in the distance which could be for anyone training in STANTA, short for Stanford Training Area we had to stand to!

In the morning we were given a 24 hrs ration pack and ate the breakfast, I know some people ate more as you could smell the evening meal tin curry around the position. We took down the ponchos and filled in the shell scraps. Cleaned around as I said you would never know we were ever there.

We fell in on the road and even though we were used to it by now started running behind the truck for several miles reaching a range I recognised from when we were here last training on Map reading. It was as I recognised the confidence course in the trees.

We lined up for the range and exercise briefing It was a serious business as this was going to be a live firing exercise across open country. We had our own instructors with us and additional DS [Drill and safety] who wore white armband. The first thing we did was line up in sections and take turns at giving fire control orders to the rest of the section locating the enemy when the targets appeared also controlling the fire. The idea was that we got the fire onto the enemy so accurate that we could advance on them by keeping them down in the trench.

The instructors in the range control room would keep the targets up until they thought we achieved that. It is now that the section machine gun GPMG comes into its own as with short two or three bursts whilst the rest of the section went forward to kill and fight through the enemy position. After that if no more enemy present reorganise in all round defence, do an ammunition count, casualty count and carry on advancing to contact. This was moved up to all the platoon on the firing point doing the same but at that increased platoon level firing in sections. It was effective training and what I had personally wanted to join the army for.

We finished mid-afternoon and doubled across to the confidence course area and a lined up in half sections in front of the various entrance holes heading underground. The entrance was made from concreate and circular like those used in underground road works, they were large enough that you had just about enough room to crawl through them in full webbing. We were though told to remove our webbing and to start crawling inside. I was thinking what's this all about. We were told that inside was a replica of a command bunker and told to start crawling in which we did at the end of the entrance it opened into a square expanse about 3m x 3m square and you could kneel upright but not stand.

After a while when everyone was crammed in the instructors started throwing in smoking gas pellets and piling webbing across the entrance holes, the game was up they were gassing us! I don't think I need to write the sheer panic and force of energy as everyone was trying to get out and into the fresh air. I realised the situation and remembering what my grandfather had told me about WW1 I removed my beret unzipped my crutch and urinated into my beret and covered my eyes nose and mouth with it and breathed very shallow breaths. When I was conscious that everyone was out, I felt my way to an exit and started to crawl out with one hand and keeping the beret tight around my face with the other.

I realised I was free, got to my feet and removed the beret. Everyone was being shouted at to put webbing back on and given a bollocking to never ever not have your gas mask with you, the lesson was learned. The Bedford truck reversed back and with much coughing and spluttering everyone was being pushed towards the truck, it was soon realised by all that I was ok, and an NCO asked me why? I explained what I had done. This was reported back to Sgt McM who I guess still had the running away from the defence position in mind held me back from the rest of the platoon who by now were on board, he then sprayed a long burst of CS gas from a can straight into my face and told the truck to set of me running blindly behind it being encouraged by the others to keep running towards the sound of their voices, I eventually had the confidence to speed up after about what must have been a hundred meters several hands grabbed me and pulled me aboard.

We drove to another range about 20 minutes away and de bussed, but as we were to slow told to get back on accompanied by lots of violent shouting and dragging and then told to get off again which we did as fast as we could again, which surprise, surprise was to slow. So again,

169

back on to shouts of who wants to go home? This lasted for about 4 or 5 get on get off's and we lined up. We had another range declaration even though we had one leaving the live firing range earlier and re fitted our BFI [Blank firing attachments] a devise that allowed the gas from the blank rounds to re cock the rifle as a live round would do.

We were issued blank rounds and formed up in all round defence in a wooded area and set up a patrol base in silence full tack, this was the night of the stag watch incident. When on sentry for the patrol base the location was at the entrance which you came to if you followed the comms cord around in any direction.

The sentry duty was always carried out in pairs staggered [Stag] so each person did an hour but changed with someone else but never at the same time. A few listening patrols went out and back but by about 01:00hrs everyone was back It was an absolute joy to get inside my sleeping bag which had been given to me by the Bedford driver along with my large pack and gas mask etc which had been handed into the guard room in camp found on the back of a Bedford truck so in fact I had not left it in Pirbright, I must have missed it with all the violence and shouting etc upon arrival.

I must have slept for about 30 mins when I was given that awful shake of the shoulder any serviceman knows accompanied by those words, "you're on stag" I then had to listen to what's is the worst sound in the world, the sleeping bag zip going down and as exhausted as you are you get yourself over to relieve the last person who just roused you and off they would go.

I did my hour and went to wake up the next person who duly came over, I then had the best sound in the world the sleeping bag zip being pulled up. I can still to this day fall asleep in minutes in any sort of position or weather! I was awaked again and told your on stag I was really shocked at how quick that two hours sleep had passed and went on stag, What no one realised is that someone to this day unknown had been turning the hands forward ten minutes here and there and getting of stag early to the extent that it was actually about 02:00hrs but the watch showing 05:00hrs and the last sentry waking everyone for stand too! The upshot was very confused instructors as to why everyone was awake and rolling up sleeping bags, stowing away kit.

The following investigation threw up no one prepared to admit it I realising I had in fact only had about 40 minutes sleep. With order restored and two watches left at the sentry position and pain of death warnings given if anymore did this type of behaviour again returned to full tack and patrol routine.

The morning stand to came and went and we had breakfast from ration packs unhindered by the instructor we had a platoon briefing and then section briefing on what is called advance to contact. The idea being we would now take the fight to the enemy after being in defence, it made sense we had a model map laid out on a poncho ground sheet showing us the various expected landmarks and enemy locations.

We broke camp again with no shouting of hassle from the instructors I think we just got it and was switched on by now and knew the drill so to speak.

We moved off as a platoon and using section platoon formations we had learnt for about four hours using arrowhead, single line, diamond formation in the various types of country which was mostly open fields with bracken. We must have patrolled about four or five miles at the very least no wonder they let us have breakfast! We eventually ended back at the range we had been on the previous day. By the range hut stood around drinking tea were several instructors Corporals and L/Sgts from the various guard's regiments all wearing white arm bands?

We did another range declaration, we handed in all our blank rounds and all our pouches' magazines were checked for blank ammunition, blank firing attachments were removed, and live ammunition handed out, 100 rounds per man, a belt of 200 rounds per man for the Gun and extra ammunition in the form of ammunition bandoliers. We had two sand filled 66MM rocket launchers and filled cases for the 84MM. We filled our water bottles, had the biscuits from the ration pack with either cheese or salmon paste when finished we had a safety briefing similar to that from the platoon section attacks the day before.

We lined up and started patrolling as a platoon forward me, RA and OI being the gun group absolutely loaded down with belts of ammunition and more in steel boxes, RA carrying the gun.

It was not long before we had the first contact as the targets came up a hundred meters or so in front of the lead section all sections going to ground, and fire control orders being shouted, as the gun group with the left section we had to go forward under suppressing fire from the others to take up a flanking position to give suppressing fire for the other sections to move forward we moved in bounds and leaps about 10 meters each time, fire a few rounds apply the safety catch on and move, and on and on until we had the gun firing in bursts of three to four rounds and the targets went down and stayed down. At the last minute the safety instructor would direct us to fire to the left of the section attacking the enemy who with much screaming and shouting would run through the enemy position bayonets fixed.

Then all around defence unless they were in depth i.e., another trench behind that and the tactics would adjust accordingly. Then all round defence and re distribute ammunition, we with the gun were always in need of ammunition, RA realising the more he fired the less we would have to carry!

This went on for ages mile after mile, we began to know when an attack was coming as we would pass the lever in the ground that the instructor following us would pull after we passed to raise the next target, most times accompanied by thunder flash grenades sticks which look like dynamite from the western films they would give of a very loud bang, These were thrown at the enemy trench to simulate grenade and 66MM Rocket fire. Occasionally members of the section would be told to lay still safety catch applied as casualties from these who we had to recover in makeshift stretchers from ponchos after the fight through and re org, thankfully as if by magic they would be made alive again and re-join their sections.

At one time RA could not see because of the very long grass and I had to go on all fours for the tripod of the gun to be rested on my back but the empty cases being ejected falling down the gap in my trousers burning the upper part of my back and the inside crack of my arse it was very painful but I could not do anything for fear of the gun being moved by my twitching and someone being killed by the movement.

I have to tell you me and OI were absolutely exhausted, on each re org the guys were getting lighter and lighter from bringing us the ammunition their job getting easier ours just the same. This went on for several miles and in the heat and sweat we were not allowed any water which really annoyed me in the re-orgs. I never knew it but the last attack we made the targets came up a good four hundred meters away. This would mean hard targeting up, down, up, down, a long way but we learnt a good lesson that the ground we were on often saved you from that and using low level dips and hidden dips we could go left or right of the enemy meaning although we were effectively under enemy fire we could walk rather than run as exhausted until no other choice that direct attack would be needed.

After this last attack in the all-round defence and re org we had to make safe meaning although we had bullets etc they were not in the breach of the weapons. We patrolled a few miles and ended at what I now know to be a place called frog hill. We made a range declaration after giving in all ammunition which in our case was not much more than two or three hundred bullets, searched pouches etc and re issued blank rounds,

On Frog hill there is a gully, and we were told to get in the gully and get a brew on nontactical. We were going to be fed by container for evening meal I certainly had nothing left in my ration pack. When the truck came, we went forward in sections mess tins out and like nervous sheep put one mess time forward for a thick stew with a pudding of sorts with custard in the other one. We went back into the gully me anyway as we walked tipping the contents of one mess tin into the other and raising it to my lips on the move guzzling it down as did the rest of using real fear the two minutes nonsense would soon start but it did not.

I remember using my finger to scrape the last residue from the tin before we were called forward to wash up the tins in a hot soapy water bucket and given sweet tea from an urn it was heaven.

Me RA and OI sat beneath this massive tree and the Scots Guards L/Sgt safety instructor who had been with us all throughout the day came over and gave us each a cigarette saying well done to us. I was grateful for that as we had worked so hard, my legs were cramping, and my bum was sore and burnt. This was in 1980, I often in reflection think about him his name unknown to me now when anything about Tumbledown comes on the television if that L/Sgt was there? I think most certainly the Scots and Welsh Guards at the depot at that time in training like me would have been. In addition, I need to add that was the hardest simulated fighting I have ever done except in Canada years later.

I cannot for a minute even begin to compare it as we had wooden targets as enemy, so none of the fear that accompanied the Parachute Regiment taking Goose Green, but from descriptions and documentaries it seems they had the same type of exhaustive repetitive attacks in the Falkland's in 1982 until daybreak. I have nothing but the utmost respect for those lads at platoon, section level they must have been completely knackered by the time the Argentine surrendered.

[In 2013 I moved back to Norfolk, a Village called Acle, I was a member of the Bisley shooting club when living in Kent, but joined another club in Norfolk who used the ranges in STANTA, after finishing shooting one day in 2014 on my way home I thought I'll go and have a look around I found the battle camp but it was run down and had been sold for development, I also found Frog Hill and parked my vehicle atop the gully walked down to the base of that tree and for reasons about RA known by me and others from the platoon I did shed a few tears as all that came rushing back and how proud I felt about what we had been at such a young age.]

The holiday was over and we got back into all round defence and in sections patrolled off using all the techniques taught, we ended up at the edge of field full of cows about midnight and you could just about make them out if they had white patches on them, as I patrolled along one cow decided to follow me and soon was nudging me in the back quite forcefully I ignored it and kept going but it came on again even more forcefully than before knocking me over falling face first in a huge pile of fresh dung, it was walking around me and I have to admit to be very frightened so I jumped to my feet and ran for my life along the side of the platoon who were in single file. I eventually got to the other side of the wire fence looking. I looked back the cow had not been chasing me as I had imagined in my mind, but what was certainly not imagined was the several kicks in my arse from an instructor asking what was I doing what was my problem? I explained and was simply dragged back at arm's length the instructor saying I needed to get a wash as I was stinking back to my section feet barley touching the ground much to the giggles of the rest of the section. To this day I will not go into a field that has cows in it.

We eventually took up a defensive position in a thick dense forest, you could hardly see your hand in front of your face and the midges were very hungry the reason for the defence position was given at the previous briefing due to an expected enemy counterattack.

We did not dig in full trenches we made what are called shell scrapes in the ground with the earth removed made into a sort of parapet about 25 inches in height and facing outwards as we were in all round defence Platoon HQ in the middle, we did not put up ponchos above us on string but simply covered ourselves with them and settles down into routine in defence.

At about 05:00hrs shortly before stand to those flares went skywards all around combined with shouts of stand to! I and everyone else could see by the light of the elimination flares the demo squad were firing and running into the defence position trying to grab people and drag them off, it was quite surreal seeing bodies intermittently fighting each other trying to stop and colleague being dragged off. As soon as this started after five minutes it stopped, we were all told to bug out which we did dragging everything with us ponchos tucked into belts and webbing straps flapping about as though we were all Batman and Robin heroes of the same name running down this dirt track for what seemed forever, the fear being if you got left behind if you could not keep up you might get lost or worse the demo squad would get you.

As day broke we mustered on the track packed up kit accounted for everyone carried out another range de brief handed over all our ammunition, checked pouches etc, made the necessary declaration to the effect we had no blank rounds pyrotechnics or parts of pyrotechnics in our possession and started a forced march at a very rapid speed down the track and out of the woods onto a main road with the instructors yelling who wanted to go home etc. How I will never know at the pace we were going we all kept together me, and EA held the gun between us me the barrel in front of RA behind me with the butt SD carrying the 84mm as though it was a toy! I always remember he was very fit lad from Devon. It became clear after about five or so miles we were heading towards the camp as we could see the military red backed signs directing as much.

I certainly know my morale went up thinking we were going to be back in camp earlier that we thought. However sure enough we went zooming straight past the gates RA stopped walking so fast causing me to have my wrist nearly disjoined by the sudden weight of the gun on my right wrist, he just kept saying fuck this, fuck this along with a few others the whole platoon had a bit of a rebellious look in their eyes when we stopped due to the discipline of the whole platoon formation untangling. With much shouting at times face to face with an instructor inches away from your own face screaming do you want to go home have you had enough goading people to say they quit RA looking like any minute he would say yes or hit someone. He looked at me and I just winked and made a mad face at him, and he laughed and knew I was going nowhere.

In the end we turned face the direction away from camp and marched on in silence, after about another mile we about turned and headed back to camp, that was it, the dreaded battle camp had ended, when we arrived back at camp we cleaned all the rifles and they were handed in to be taken back by the Bedford truck with baggage and an escort to Pirbright.

We ate the heartiest of breakfasts of course accompanied by the two minutes ruling and screams of instructors to chuck what you had not eaten in the swill bins. A hot shower, shave, cleaned polished boots and change into lightweight trousers spare combat jacket and on the truck to Thetford station for the train back to Brookwood via Liverpool Street and Waterloo. When we were in public the instructors were like angels around us if butter would not melt in their mouths. I don't remember much about the return trip like everyone else within minutes on board the train I slept the sleep of the dead.

Chapter XIII

March and shoot.

Passing out Parade 8th August 1980.

The culmination of all the fitness training and techniques to get over the various obstacles on the assault course, followed by a platoon shoot at scored targets is known as the march and shoot.

You must pass this as an individual within and as a platoon to get out of the depot. As with everything in the guards it starts with an inspection.

We had a pre inspection of all our kit on the road outside our accommodation block before marching up to the drill shed on the main square. We were in full CEFO, helmets and sand filled 66mm rockets the same with the cases for the 84mm, we had drill grenades and at the drill sheds issues 100 rounds of live ammunition each 20 in each magazine. We also had 200 rounds belted ammunition for each person for the gun. I had 400 rounds belted for the gun RA had 200. We had everything down to spare boot laces and housewife, [sowing kit] the home made no military issue id cards top left breast pocket of the combat jacket, notebook and pencil sharped at both ends.

We had to step forward and have our water bottles filled from a jerry can under inspection in a line. Then once put away over to the next que to have your webbing weighed, I think it was circa 25Lbs from there join the three ranks and every other Junior Guardsman had to step back and take out an item and show it; for me I remember it was my green army towel which was wrapped around my smaller mess tin contents every time there was a discrepancy a point from however many points I don't actually remember was taken of the platoon and you as an individual if you were the offender.

You then had to place all your magazines on the floor and show your pouches were empty of any other ammunition replace put all the kit on an inspection was conducted of the weapons to ensure no magazines were fitted and no rounds in the chamber. We then filed forward and had to make several jumps up and down to show no noise was coming from you or the kit if so you lost a point for the platoon and yourself if any noise was found you had to remove the kit and sort out what it was before getting on the Bedford truck.

We then went by road out through the depot to what is called the impact area. I had only ever been there once when we fired the 84mm it was also near the grenade range. In the distance from where we de bussed we saw the incredibly old and rusted tanks used for target practice. We got into three ranks and the PTI took out the stopwatch and off we went, it was about a mile to the start of a single-track way next to the fence that I assume keeps people out of that area this track led to what is known as the four sisters.

The four sisters are a series of very steep hills with an equally deep valley between them the end of one was the start of the other each top to top about 300m in distance, but it was the steep inclines that were painful thankfully followed by the ease of running down the valley. I think the total distance of the whole course from the impact area to the start of the assault course was circa 4-5 miles, opinions vary, in any case, it was a tough course even without full kit. I am aware that various platoons in the past had set record times and scores but no one I can remember had the remotest interest in trying for a record time just to pass.

I had agreed as we had practiced before with RA to take the gun from the start of the first of the sister and carry it to the end of the first of the four he would take it from the top of number two to the top of number three and so on and so forth at the bottom of the fourth I was completely exhausted legs like jelly being sick I thought I was finished; but in my mind I thought how can I give up now? I thought of my grandfather in WWI 1918 as young as me winning the Military Medal at Riqueval bridge St. Quentin France

I gritted my teeth and with an internal scream created what I have only ever experienced twice in my life, both times on this day, what is called second breath or wind, basically a huge adrenalin rush I was up and over the top of the fourth sister pushing RA waiting to take the gun aside as I was not in the least bit tired; Quite the opposite. I had the energy of twenty men I could not go fast enough I felt absolutely no pain at all, I was passing others who were all struggling to keep going, we had as explained before run these hills so we all knew what was coming and I recognised the slight single track bend to the left that meant we were on the last leg, in front of me was SD from Devon [now lives in Australia] with the 88mm plus the two shells his number two should have been carrying his own rifle and his number twos rifle bounding along as though on a 100m race, SD was incredibly fit and a 20 a day smoker!

The effects of the adrenaline rush came to an end as I was in all round defence circle leg over leg, I could hear the heavy breathing of everyone eventually RA came and lay beside me taking the gun, a look of sheer desperation on his face, like everyone he was chin strapped.

We moved off in our rehearsed places and went to the first of the many obstacles and worked our way through them again SD another extremely fit Junior Guardsman setting the example on the highest of the walls by sheer strength with some assistance pulling themselves to the top then pulling each person over whilst staying at the top. At the end of each obstacle, we went into all round defence in silence always conscious of the PTIs and other NCOs with their clip boards deducting points for helmets coming off or not doing the obstacle which was no one we all had practised so often we had it down.

The only obstacle I knew I could not make as did several others was what is called the monkey bars, this looks like a set of ladders placed horizontal above a pool of filthy stagnant green water. I had accepted that I would go into the water I would simply take the deducted personal points for doing so. I always fell in on all the practice no matter what technique or coaching I used, my upper body strength was just not up to it.

As we knelt in all round defence prior to going over it I again gritted my teeth had that internal scream and was at the bars as soon as my turn came like a mad man in my mind swinging my arms back and forth saying to myself in a rage left right left right every other bar as my hands moved forward bar after bar, before I knew it I was across I simply could not believe it, RA came across with the gun to the all-round defence and just winked at me.

The assault course finished.

We then ran down as a platoon to the start of the range and took up a position on the firing point that we had practiced many times throughout that year me and RA in the first trench as you came upon the range RA got behind the gun, I waited to feed the first of the 200 round belts of ammunition across the feed tray the cover held open by RA.

As we were waiting to get our breath others in the platoon ran past, they dropped off their own linked belt of 200 rounds they had been carrying for the gun by my feet. As soon as we were all in position the command load, ready, watch and shoot, watch and shoot came. We had targets on point 1 and 2 that were triple 11 targets basically the target was the height and width of a man, but we had two sets of three one on each point.

The targets were at three hundred meters RA fired in burst of two to three rounds I could see his lips moving as he was saying 99, 99, 99 each time he pulled and let go of the trigger I watched for the fall of the rounds and if ok I would tap his left shoulder if he was too high I would point with my right had upwards or the opposite for two low. He was on the ball. The targets went down I clipped another belt of 200 to the one still sticking out of the housing, targets came up again and we carried on the same only this time switching to the targets on point 2. This went on for quite some time RA getting more accurate as time went past as his breathing became less laboured between targets appearing and going down.

The targets went down by being run by Junior Guardsmen in the butts [the safe area behind the targets] they would pull the targets up when ordered and take them down under the same. In the platoon itself no one was registered against a target so as planned those who were not very good shots would only fire one magazine throughout and those who were good shots fired all if needs be there ammunition. The idea being that at the end of the shoot all the hits would be counted and added to your points, in addition any ammunition we did not use each round

183

given back was a point gained so it better to have those not so good shots do not waste ammunition. I don't think this is cheating just playing to our strengths!

Finally, the shoot was over, we unloaded, we had fired through the gun 600 rounds in what seemed no time at all. After unloading we queued up to hand in our ammunition and made a range declaration and checked the weapons. The hits on target were being counted in the butts a sort of conference was held in the range hut all of us nervously waiting, a Land Rover had come with an urn of hot milky tea. I remember how excellent it tasted and wanted a second mug. I guess I was like everyone, I was dehydrated those who had fallen into the various water obstacles were stood with clouds of steam coming off them like boiling kettles!

In any case the senior PTI came out and gave us the good news we had passed, and no individual had failed. That was it, that was the last thing we had to pass other than the actual passing out parade itself. That was a dreaded test over and now we were on the last steps to becoming qualified Guardsman, moreover, the privilege of wearing the bearskin cap with a red plume.

I remember distinctly as we marched past the cinema, which was not far from the range, we used on our way back to our room how proud I felt, not just of myself but of everyone. I was starting to cramp up in my calf muscles as did a few others, so we ended up doing a combination of doubling, [running] and walking back through the depot with our heads held very high, for once no shouting or screaming from the instructors.

It was done.

Over the next few days, we spent most of the time on the drill square with the other platoons practicing for the passing out parade scheduled for the 8$^{th of}$ August, this was just shy of a year at the depot training. All our Number 2 dress uniforms were pressed in the Hoffman press room they had creases you could cut a loaf of bread with. We had the platoon photo taken which is included in this book.

The night before passing out I was like a child before Christmas. The evening was spent going over our kit, we were immaculate not a loose thread or whitening on a single piece of brass where it should not be.

I rightly felt immensely proud as we marched past the commandant and gave him eyes right! the parade was great; we had the band and the corps of drums playing it was like a mini trooping of the colour. It felt very odd seeing my family walk into the drill sheds and taking their seats I could see them from where we were forming up by the Gym some way off, but I recognised the old man's walk.

I was really surprised they had made it, moreover they were on time! a miracle. After the parade we had chance to have a beer and sandwich with my parents meeting the instructors, my father ever the socialist was making mutterings about the officers and their cut-glass aristocratic voices I kept him away from Mr Dobson.

By mid-afternoon everything was packed away for leave, the instructors had a chat with us all with tips about Battalion life. All of them were agreed on one thing and that was those of us who were going to the second Battalion, if possible, to try and not get posted to Number four company if you could help it.

Yep, that's where I ended up…

58 Pattern webbing minus gas mask pouch quite good until it got wet and shrunk.

Left magazine pouch, water bottle and mug pouch, two kidney pouches held mess tins, Right Magazine pouch underneath poncho holder.

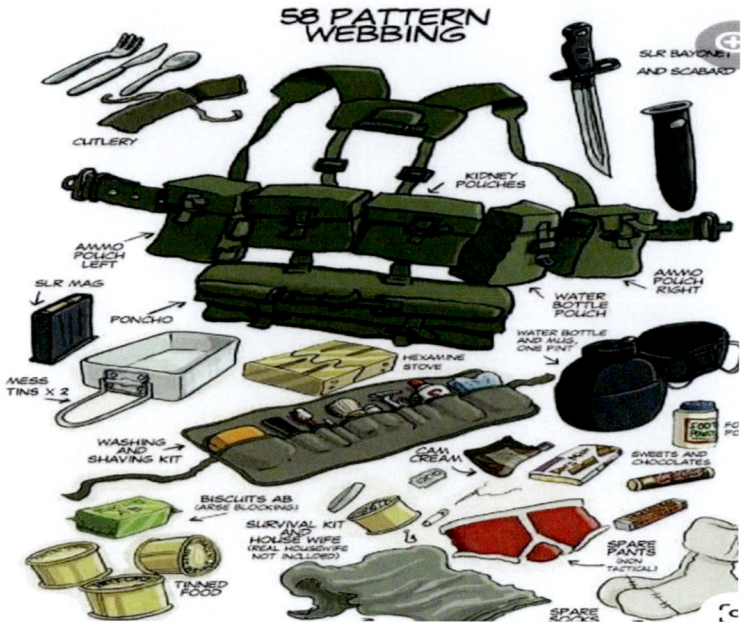

The basic contents of CEFO minus ammunition gas mask pouch

A series of photographs of Gibralter two passing out parade. I am first person you see, to my left HW behind him TR, next to him red sash Sgt R McC behind me EM behind him PR next him HT just out of picture, BI all marching off the square as Gurdsmen.

I am 3rd from the right front rank.

Me centre of picture

189

Gibraltar two pre passing out photograph Circa August 1980

GIBRALTAR TWO — N? COMPANY

Epilogue

We returned to the Depot from our post passing out leave mid-September 1980 almost a year to the day we arrived. We were now called TS, trained soldiers around the Depot and could drink in the bar! we were there awaiting our postings to the First Battalion based in Fallingbostal West Germany, basically soldiers in armoured personal carries. The Second Battalion which was in Caterham Barracks Surrey in the old Guards depot barracks, performing ceremonial duties such as Buckingham palace Guard, Tower of London Guard, St James palace Guard, Trooping the colour, State opening of parliament, and Guards of Honor for state visitors from around the world.

I wanted to go to Germany so I chose the Second Battalion although they were in Caterham now, in December 1980 through to the end of January 1981 the Battalions would be swapping locations. This meant that I would get four months performing ceremonial duties which I was quite looking forward to.

The following went to the First Battalion.

Gdsm A.C from Coventry
Gdsm B.R from Peterborough
Gdsm E.G from Warminster
Gdsm H.L from Doncaster
Gdsm L.SY from Essex
Gdsm L.ST from Coventry
Gdsm M.N from Sheffield
Gdsm R.A from Cornwall
Gdsm V.R from Germany

The following went to the Second Battalion.

Gdsm B.G from Essex
Gdsm C.G from Cornwall
Gdsm D.S from Birmingham
Gdsm F.G from Norfolk
Gdsm H.A from Cornwall
Gdsm S.R from Tyne & Wear
Gdsm S.M from Warwickshire
Gdsm T.R from Leicester
Gdsm W.D from Essex

Continuation training Guards Depot Corps of Drums.

Drummer D.S from Sussex
Drummer E.I from Devon
Drummer O.R from Newcastle upon Tyne
Drummer O.I from Shirley
Drummer S.D from Devon
Drummer W.P from Coventry

I served in Caterham Barracks from 27 September 1980 to 8 December 1981.

I know the dates for two reasons the first is the day we arrived in West Germany John Lennon had been shot in New York. The second is all the dates are listed in my record of service book, or [Red Book] as it's known.

The book is given to you upon leaving the Army to show potential employers your skills and attributes. The Army by all accounts have become much, much better at what you have in the way of transferable skills into civilian life now than when I left, for example in my Red Book I am listed as follows.

"Suitable to be a petrol pump attendant requiring minimal supervision!"

I served in West Germany from January 1981 to 1984 whilst there I went to Canada twice, and an operational tour of West Belfast in 1982.

In 1984 I left West Germany and was stationed in Chelsea Barracks performing ceremonial duties. We moved from the tumbling down Chelsea Barracks to the newly rebuilt Wellington Barracks in 1985.

In 1985 I got married to the first Mrs Fish of which eventually there would be three.

In 1986 I changed Battalions from the Second Battalion to the First Battalion based in Caterham Surrey and after a few months I went with the First Battalion to Hong Kong. I had my first child a boy named Martin whilst we were there. I was the happiest I have ever been in my entire life those two years in Hong Kong, it was the most wonderful posting.

I returned to the UK with the First Battalion in January 1987 to Wellington Barracks.

The First Battalion went to Kenya on exercise in 1988, I enjoyed the country it was I felt easy to understand why the whites never wanted to leave.

In March 1989, my daughter Emma was born whilst I was in London in married quarters in Putney. My marriage to Mrs Fish Number one was falling apart and affecting me mentally more than I realised at the time, we separated.

In 1991 I went to the first Gulf war with the First Battalion.

In 1992 The First Battalion went to Munster in West Germany. I did not want to go and asked to stay in the UK and transfer over to the Second Battalion, the main reason was due to the breakup of my marriage and the effect upon my children.

However, I was posted in 1992 back to West Germany in Oxford Barracks Munster.

The Armed forces around that time were going to go through a period of change and reorganisation, it became clear that we the Coldstream Guards along with one Battalion from each Guards Regiment would soon be dis-banded.

In our case the Coldstream Guards the Second Battalion based in Chelsea Barracks was chosen to be disbanded in 1993.

I was very unhappy in Munster due to the situation of my Children in the UK and reduced my rank voluntarily to get a cross posting back to the UK and the Second Battalion. It was whilst with the Second Battalion I went to Kenya a second time.

I left the Army from Chelsea Barracks just short of the disbandment on 10 October 1993. I had served 15years 71 days in total. I was asked if I had anything to say before I left to the Commanding officer? I said very emotionally yes, "that, leaving the regiment was equally as difficult to do as joining it in the first place and going through the Guards depot."

The Commanding officer wished me well and reminded me that the regiment was a family, I should join my local association to stay connected I could always reach out for help from the association if I needed it. As I type, I have been for the last 5 years the secretary of the Coldstream Guards Association Norwich Branch.

I had worked part time for a year in security whilst serving in the First and then Second Battalions in London during the evenings, weekends and leave periods. It was by which means I saved enough money for a deposit on a one bed flat in London Surrey Quays. I did not want to be that Guardsman at 30 who left the barracks with only the clothes he stood up in and move back home to his old room with mum and dad! Believe me it happens.

I had a very brief but very financially rewarding career as a trainee Bund broker on the German desk of a financial institute on Fenchurch Street until I punched one of the other employees and was asked to leave. I had only lasted 5 months as a civilian and already been sacked.

I then started my own Potato round; I was selling potatoes by the sack door to door in all the high unemployment and single mother areas around London, it was a roaring success. I eventually had to buy another van and employ two Irishmen to do re delivering to the established customers whilst I started to approach and undercut the local suppliers to Fish and Chip shops, pubs, cafes etc.

I had to rent a storage unit in Crystal palace as I was having so many tons of potatoes delivered by arctic truck from Lincolnshire too keep up. In the end I had to give it up as foolishly against advice from the two Irish lads I employed an accountant and within weeks the tax office and the Child support agency were making life unbearable. I simply packed it in. I had though made enough money in the 9 months to pay of 80 per cent of my mortgage.

I then accepted a job working for a friend who ran a security company the same one I had been with whilst serving, he was ex Grenadier Guards and we got on well.

I stayed in the security industry working for the corps of Commissionaires in the national control room, a job that taught me how to use a computer, more so get some much-needed confidence in myself. I met and married Mrs Fish Number two in 1996 and had a second Son called Stephen.

In 1997 I got a job as a driver trainee telecoms technician with Orange. I became a team leader and Manager whilst there.

In 2007 I started adult college part time evening study in Kent on an Access to Teaching Course.

In 2009 I got a job in BT as an Operations Manager.

In 2010 I graduated from Birkbeck university of London BA Hons in History.

In 2013 I got a job as a Service Delivery Manager in Ericsson and moved back to Norfolk as the job was work from home.

In 2016 I left Ericsson to start teacher training whilst working in a primary school.

I retired in 2018 after a year and a few months working via an agency as a supply teacher or HLTA Higher level teaching assistant. I only lasted as a retiree a couple of months as I was going stir crazy.

In 2018 I started working for the Ministry of Justice in the probation service as an administrator.

In 2024 I started training to become a probation service officer which I am still doing as I type.

I keep in contact with many who I trained with and who trained me in Gibraltar two, sadly some have passed away, others have moved as far away as Australia and New Zealand. I am now sixty, I am glad I wrote this as daily I see in social media that many a former Coldstreamer sadly passing away, I could be next!

Photo taken the day I left the Coldstream Guards October 1993

198

I understand that thousands of ex Guardsmen regardless of former rank and Regiment will read this and have experiences happen to them at the depot that we in Gibraltar two did or did not have that I have forgotten.

.

Sgt R McM this picture was taken I think in 1994 when he was the WO1 (ACSM). He went on to become a commissioned officer himself. He was, and still is held in extremely high esteem by all those who served under him, and alongside him. A soldier through and through, both on the Drill square, and in the field. We were so lucky to have had him as our Platoon Sergeant for that year.

L/Sgt TB instructed us in Drill SAA in the field both squads. He has a fantastic send of humour, said the funniest things on drill and in the field.

L/Sgt MC picture taken from squad pass out photo 1980 He taught Drill of course, to the other squad not mine, he was the Instructor for SAA and also in the field.

A very strict disciplinarian.

L/Sgt TC, picture taken from squad pass out photo 1980. He taught
Drill of course; he was my squad instructor for SAA and in the
field.

He was of course though at home on the drill square, but he really
knew his stuff in the field, seemed to me to be more a field soldier.

L/Sgt HK taken in 1996 as the RSM of the Apprentice College Harrogate. L/Sgt HK was my Drill instructor, it goes without saying he was also an excellent soldier in the field.

Also, an excellent Rugby player.

Equipment layout in gaol

J L/Cpl CA

J /Gdsm LD

J /Gdsm S

J/Sgt WD

On the Left J /Gdsm RS, the first Geordie I ever met in person, it took me ages to understand a word he said.

On the right is J /Gdsm HT from Cornwall, both pictures taken a while after the depot as both have been to NI

JUNIOR ARMY RATES OF PAY WITH EFFECT FROM 1 APRIL 1980

AGE	16-16½ years	16½ - 17 years	17-17½ years	Over 17½ years
Gross weekly entitlement.	£39.27	£43.82	£55.27	£70.42
Less:				
Food and accom. charges.	£11.55	£11.55	£11.55	£10.75
Tax and Ins.	£ 6.25	£ 7.50	£10.60	£16.10
Total Deductions	£17.80	£19.05	£22.15	£26.35
NET AVAILABLE WEEKLY PAY.	£21.47	£24.77	£33.12	£44.07

On attaining 18 years of age the rate of pay to which entitled will be determined by the length of service to which the soldier is committed as an adult -

        i.e.   Scale A -   3 years
                     Scale B -   6 years
                     Scale C -   9 years

Unemployment benefit in 1980 for a 16-year-old was £26.00 per week!

Grenade range Pirbright